UNITED STATES ARMY

Infantry, Armor/Cavalry, Artillery Battalions

1957-2011

Timothy S. Aumiller
Sunbury, Pennsylvania

0-9776072-2-4

Tiger Lily Publications
A division of General Data LLC
Takoma Park, Maryland 20912
v.1.0 March19, 2008

THIS BOOK IS DEDICATED BY THE AUTHOR TO THE

SOLDIERS OF THE UNITED STATES ARMY

WHEREVER THEY SERVE IN THE GLOBAL WAR ON TERROR

AND PARTICULARLY THOSE IN

AFGHANISTAN AND IRAQ.

THERE ARE THOSE, I KNOW, WHO WILL SAY THAT THE LIBERATION OF
HUMANITY, THE FREEDOM OF MAN AND MIND, IS NOTHING BUT A DREAM. THEY
ARE RIGHT. IT IS THE AMERICAN DREAM.

~ARCHIBALD MACLEISH~

Contents

Infantry Battalions 1957-2011 p.1

Artillery Battalions (Field & Air Defense) 1957-2011 p.47

Armor & Cavalry Battalions 1957-2011 p.114

<u>Acronyms</u>

AD Air Defense
ADA Air Defense Artillery
T Training Battalion
FA Field Artillery Battalions
FA Sqd Field Artillery Squadron
Sup Sqd Support Squadron
RSTA Reconnaissance, Surveillance, Target Acquisition Squadron

I. Infantry Battalions 1957-2011

1st Infantry Regiment-Active Component

1-1	United States Military Academy	5-1-1958	Present
2-1	2nd Infantry Division	6-14-1958	5-10-1963
	196th Infantry Brigade	9-15-1965	2-15-1969
	23rd Infantry Division	2-15-1969	11-30-1971
	196th Infantry Brigade	11-30-1971	7-21-1972
	9th Infantry Division	7-21-1972	2-16-1991
	199th Infantry Brigade	2-16-1991	1-14-1994
	6th Infantry Division	12-16-1995	4-17-1998
	172nd Infantry Brigade	4-17-1998	11-16-2006
	2nd Infantry Division	11-16-2006	Present
3-1	77th Infantry Division	5-1-1959	3-26-1963
	11th Infantry Brigade	7-1-1966	2-15-1969
	23rd Infantry Division	2-15-1969	11-30-1971
	9th Infantry Division	3-16-1988	2-16-1991
4-1	6th Infantry Division	11-24-1967	7-24-1968
	Fort Campbell Kentucky	7-24-1968	7-21-1969
5-1	6th Infantry Division	7-24-1967	7-24-1968
	Fort Campbell Kentucky	7-24-1968	7-21-1969
6-1	6th Infantry Division	7-24-1967	7-24-1968
	Fort Campbell Kentucky	7-24-1968	7-21-1969

2nd Infantry Regiment-Active Component

1-2	5th Infantry Division	2-19-1962	7-15-1965
	1st Infantry Division	7-15-1965	2-23-1983
2-2	1st Infantry Division	2-15-1957	2-28-1959
	24th Infantry Division	2-28-1959	2-19-1962
	5th Infantry Division	2-19-1962	7-12-1965
	1st Infantry Division	7-12-1965	4-15-1970
	9th Infantry Division	3-21-1973	5-15-1991
	1st Infantry Division	2-16-1996	- -2006
	1st Infantry Division	4-17-2007	Present
3-2	83rd Infantry Division	3-20-1959	12-31-1965
4-2	83rd Infantry Division	4-15-1963	12-31-1965

3rd Infantry Regiment-Active Component

1-3	Fort Myer Virginia	7-1-1957	Present
2-3	7th Infantry Division	7-1-1957	7-1-1963
	199th Infantry Brigade	6-1-1966	10-15-1970
	2nd Infantry Division	3-16-2000	Present
3-3	103rd Infantry Division	5-18-1959	3-15-1963
	205th Infantry Brigade	3-15-1963	8-15-1994
4-3	11th Infantry Brigade	7-1-1966	2-15-1969
	23rd Infantry Division	2-15-1969	11-30-1971
5-3	6th Infantry Division	11-24-1967	7-24-1968
	Fort Campbell Kentucky	7-24-1968	7-21-1969
6-3	6th Infantry Division	7-24-1968	7-24-1968
	Fort Campbell Kentucky	7-24-1968	2-1-1969
7-3	6th Infantry Division	11-24-1967	7-25-1968
H-3	Fort Myer Virginia	9-10-1971	Present

4th Infantry Regiment-Active Component

1-4	2nd Infantry Brigade	2-15-1958	4-18-1963
	3rd Infantry Division	6-5-1963	12-16-1987
	Germany	11-16-1990	Present
2-4	3rd Infantry Division	2-15-1958	4-18-1963
	Germany	4-18-1963	12-16-1987
	56th Field Artillery Command	7-21-1969	6-30-1991
	10th Infantry Division	1-16-2005	Present
3-4	102nd Infantry Division	6-1-1959	12-31-1965

5th Infantry Regiment-Active Component

1-5	8th Infantry Division	8-1-1957	2-1-1959
	1st Infantry Division	2-1-1959	2-1-1963
	25th Infantry Division	2-1-1963	1-16-1986
	2nd Infantry Division	4-16-1987	8-16-1995
	25th Infantry Division	8-16-1995	6-1-2006
	25th Infantry Division	12-16-2006	Present
2-5	9th Infantry Division	12-1-1957	1-31-1962
	25th Infantry Division	12-6-1969	12-15-1970
	25th Infantry Division	8-16-1995	11-16-2005
3-5	94th Infantry Division	5-1-1959	3-1-1963
	193rd Infantry Brigade	6-26-1968	10-1-1983

6th Infantry Regiment-Active Component

1-6	1st Armored Division	2-15-1957	5-12-1967
	198th Infantry Brigade	5-12-1967	2-15-1969
	23rd Infantry Division	2-15-1969	11-30-1971
	1st Armored Division	9-13-1972	1-17-1992
	3rd Infantry Division	1-17-1992	2-15-1996
	1st Armored Division	2-16-1997	Present
2-6	Berlin Germany	6-1-1958	9-1-1963
	Berlin Brigade	9-1-1963	6-29-1984
	1st Armored Division	8-1-1984	1-17-1992
	3rd Infantry Division	1-17-1992	8-16-1992
	1st Armored Division	2-16-1997	Present
3-6	Berlin Germany	6-1-1958	9-1-1963
	Berlin Brigade	9-1-1963	6-29-1984
	5th Infantry Division	- -1985	12-15-1992
4-6	102nd Infantry Division	6-1-1959	12-31-1965
	Berlin Brigade	9-13-1972	6-29-1984
	5th Infantry Division	- -1985	12-15-1992
	2nd Armored Division	12-15-1992	8-16-1993
5-6	1st Armored Division	2-3-1962	5-10-1971
	5th Infantry Division	- -1985	12-15-1992
6-6	102nd Infantry Division	4-1-1963	12-31-1965
	1st Armored Division	6-16-1987	1-17-1992
7-6	1st Armored Division	5-12-1967	10-20-1967
	2nd Armored Division	10-20-1967	12-15-1970
	1st Armored Division	11-16-1987	1-17-1992

7th Infantry Regiment-Active Component

1-7	3rd Infantry Division	7-1-1957	12-15-1992
2-7	10th Infantry Division	7-1-1957	6-14-1958
	3rd Infantry Division	6-20-1963	5-1-1966
	24th Infantry Division	12-16-1987	2-16-1996
	3rd Infantry Division	2-16-1996	Present
3-7	102nd Infantry Division	6-1-1959	4-1-1963
	199th Infantry Brigade	6-1-1966	10-15-1970
	197th Infantry Brigade	3-21-1973	10-16-1987
	24th Infantry Division	12-16-1987	2-16-1996
	3rd Infantry Division	2-16-1996	Present
4-7	Fort Benning Georgia	9-24-1962	2-15-1963
	3rd Infantry Division	12-16-1987	5-15-1992

4

8th Infantry Regiment-Active Component

1-8	4th Infantry Division	4-1-1957	4-15-1970
	4th Infantry Division	9-13-1972	Present
2-8	8th Infantry Division	8-1-1957	1-1-1959
	1st Infantry Division	1-1-1959	10-1-1963
	4th Infantry Division	10-1-1963	9-13-1972
	4th Infantry Division	8-1-1984	12-15-1989
	4th Infantry Division	12-15-1995	Present
3-8	4th Infantry Division	10-1-1963	12-15-1970
	8th Infantry Division	8-1-1984	10-16-1991
4-8	8th Infantry Division	8-1-1984	10-16-1991
	1st Armored Division	10-16-1991	2-16-1997
E-8	Rosendale Massachusetts	3-22-1963	12-17-1965
5-8	8th Infantry Division	6-16-1986	10-16-1991

9th Infantry Regiment-Active Component

1-9	2nd Infantry Division	6-20-1957	12-16-1957
	Fort Wainwright Alaska	12-16-1957	1-25-1963
	2nd Infantry Division	1-25-1963	4-16-1987
	7th Infantry Division	7-16-1987	8-16-1995
	2nd Infantry Division	8-16-1995	Present
2-9	2nd Infantry Division	6-14-1958	6-27-1971
	2nd Infantry Division	8-15-1975	12-15-1979
	7th Infantry Division	4-29-1983	8-16-1995
	2nd Infantry Division	8-16-1995	Present
3-9	102nd Infantry Division	6-1-1959	12-31-1965
	7th Infantry Division	1-25-1983	8-16-1995
4-9	Fort Wainwright Alaska	1-25-1963	5-20-1963
	171st Infantry Brigade	5-20-1963	1-14-1966
	25th Infantry Division	1-14-1966	6-5-1972
	172nd Infantry Brigade	8-2-1972	1-6-1983
	7th Infantry Division	4-29-1983	4-16-1987
	6th Infantry Division	4-16-1987	12-15-1995
	2nd Infantry Division	6-1-2006	Present
5-9	102nd Infantry Division	4-1-1963	12-31-1965
	6th Infantry Division	11-16-1987	12-15-1995
6-9	171st Infantry Brigade	12-20-1965	11-13-1972
	6th Infantry Division	11-16-1987	1-17-1994

10th Infantry Regiment-Active Component

1-10	Fort Ord California		6-1-1957	4-25-1961
	5th Infantry Division		2-19-1962	12-15-1970
	4th Infantry Division		12-15-1970	6-16-1989
	Fort Leonard Wood Missouri	T	4-15-1996	10-16-1999
2-10	10th Infantry Division		7-1-1957	6-14-1958
	Fort William Davis Canal Zone		4-23-1961	2-19-1962
	5th Infantry Division		2-19-1962	12-15-1970
	4th Infantry Division		12-15-1970	3-21-1973
	Fort Leonard Wood Missouri	T	6-4-1987	1-31-2007
	187th Infantry Brigade	T	1-31-2007	5-17-2007
	3rd Chemical Brigade	T	5-17-2007	Present
3-10	83rd Infantry Division		3-20-1959	12-31-1965
	5th Infantry Division		5-26-1967	12-15-1970
	5th Infantry Division		11-26-1967	8-1-1984
	Fort Leonard Wood Missouri	T	6-4-1987	1-31-2007
	187th Infantry Brigade	T	1-31-2007	5-17-2007
	3rd Chemical Brigade	T	5-17-2007	Present
4-10	Fort William Davis Canal Zone		2-19-1962	10-1-1962
	193rd Infantry Brigade		10-1-1962	10-1-1983
	Fort Leonard Wood Missouri	T	6-4-1987	Present
5-10	5th Infantry Division	T	6-4-1987	4-15-1996
6-10	Fort Leonard Wood Missouri	T	6-4-1987	4-15-1996

11th Infantry Regiment-Active Component

1-11	2nd Infantry Division		6-14-1958	2-19-1962
	5th Infantry Division		2-19-1962	8-27-1971
	4th Infantry Division		9-13-1972	1-15-1984
	Fort Benning Georgia	T	8-14-1987	6-27-2007
	199th Infantry Brigade	T	6-27-2007	Present
2-11	5th Infantry Division		2-15-1962	12-15-1970
	4th Infantry Division		12-15-1970	6-1-1972
	Fort Benning Georgia	T	8-14-1987	6-27-2007
3-11	83rd Infantry Division		3-20-1959	12-31-1965
	5th Infantry Division		5-26-1967	12-15-1970
	4th Infantry Division		12-15-1970	8-6-1971
	5th Infantry Division		8-27-1977	8-1-1984
	Fort Benning Georgia	T	8-14-1987	6-27-2007

6

	199th Infantry Brigade	T	6-27-2007	Present
4-11	83rd Infantry Division		4-15-1963	12-31-1965
5-11	5th Infantry Division		11-15-1969	12-15-1970

12th Infantry Regiment-Active Component

1-12	4th Infantry Division		4-1-1957	Present
2-12	8th Infantry Division		8-1-1957	3-24-1959
	1st Infantry Division		3-24-1959	10-1-1963
	4th Infantry Division		10-1-1963	8-1-1967
	25th Infantry Division		8-1-1967	4-17-1971
	4th Infantry Division		4-1-1976	9-21-1976
	4th Infantry Division		6-16-1989	9-15-1995
			9-29-2005	Present
3-12	79th Infantry Division		3-22-1959	3-28-1963
	4th Infantry Division		11-1-1965	12-15-1970
	8th Infantry Division		6-16-1989	10-16-1991
	1st Armored Division		10-16-1991	2-15-1997
4-12	199th Infantry Brigade		6-1-1966	10-15-1970
	8th Infantry Division		6-16-1989	10-16-1991
	1st Armored Division		10-16-1991	2-15-1997
5-12	Fort Lewis Washington		11-1-1967	4-7-1968
	199th Infantry Brigade		4-7-1968	10-15-1970

13th Infantry Regiment-Active Component

1-13	8th Infantry Division		8-1-1957	2-28-1959
	1st Infantry Division		2-28-1959	4-25-1963
	8th Infantry Division		4-25-1963	6-16-1989
	Fort Jackson South Carolina	T	11-16-2005	1-31-2007
	193rd Infantry Brigade	T	1-31-2007	Present
2-13	9th Infantry Division		12-1-1957	1-31-1962
	8th Infantry Division		4-1-1963	8-1-1984
	Fort Jackson South Carolina	T	2-27-1987	1-31-2007
	193rd Infantry Brigade	T	1-31-2007	Present
3-13	94th Infantry Division		5-1-1959	3-1-1963
	Fort Jackson South Carolina	T	2-27-1987	1-31-2007
	193rd Infantry Brigade	T	1-31-2007	Present
4-13	198th Infantry Brigade		5-10-1967	5-12-1967
	Fort Jackson South Carolina	T	2-27-1987	Present

14th Infantry Regiment-Active Component

1-14	25th Infantry Division	2-1-1957	8-1-1967
	4th Infantry Division	8-1-1967	12-15-1970
	25th Infantry Division	12-15-1970	Present
2-14	Fort Benning Georgia	5-25-1957	7-1-1958
	1st Infantry Brigade	7-1-1958	5-16-1960
	25th Infantry Division	8-26-1963	6-5-1972
	10th Infantry Division	12-19-1985	Present
3-14	102nd Infantry Division	6-1-1959	12-31-1965
	25th Infantry Division	12-6-1969	12-15-1970
	10th Infantry Division	3-2-1986	4-16-1996
D-14	Virgin Islands	8-17-1959	3-31-1968
4-14	10th Infantry Division	3-2-1986	
E-14	South Korea	12-24-1960	1-1-1966
	South Vietnam	6-30-1971	11-20-1971
5-14	25th Infantry Division	9-16-1986	8-16-1995

15th Infantry Regiment-Active Component

1-15	3rd Infantry Division	7-1-1957	1-17-1992
	3rd Infantry Division	2-16-1996	
2-15	10th Infantry Division	7-1-1957	6-14-1958
	3rd Infantry Division	6-1-1963	2-15-1996
3-15	63rd Infantry Division	6-1-1959	12-31-1965
	24th Infantry Division	8-25-1989	2-16-1996
	3rd Infantry Division	2-16-1996	Present
4-15	63rd Infantry Division	4-1-1963	12-31-1965
	194th Armored Brigade	6-16-1987	- -1990
5-15	3rd Infantry Division	6-16-1987	2-16-1996

16th Infantry Division-Active Component

1-16	1st Infantry Division	2-15-1957	3-13-1959
	8th Infantry Division	3-13-1959	4-1-1963
	1st Infantry Division	4-1-1963	Present
2-16	1st Infantry Division	10-1-1963	8-17-1974
	1st Infantry Division	5-1-1976	9-21-1976
	1st Infantry Division	12-16-1979	2-16-1996
	1st Infantry Division	1-16-2006	Present

3-16	94th Infantry Division	5-1-1959	1-7-1963
	187th Infantry Brigade	1-7-1963	4-15-1994
4-16	1st Infantry Division	2-23-1983	7-15-1991
5-16	1st Infantry Division	2-23-1983	7-15-1991

17th Infantry Regiment-Active Component

1-17	7th Infantry Division	7-1-1957	4-2-1971
	2nd Infantry Division	4-2-1971	8-16-1986
	6th Infantry Division	11-16-1986	1-17-1994
	6th Infantry Division	2-17-1994	4-17-1998
	172nd Infantry Brigade	4-17-1998	11-16-2006
	2nd Infantry Division	11-16-2006	Present
2-17	7th Infantry Division	2-1-1963	4-2-1971
	7th Infantry Division	4-21-1975	4-25-1983
	6th Infantry Division	11-16-1987	10-16-1989
3-17	103rd Infantry Division	5-18-1959	3-15-1963
	205th Infantry Brigade	3-15-1963	1-31-1968
	7th Infantry Division	10-21-1975	8-15-1993
D-17	South Korea	6-24-1960	12-26-1964
	Frankfort Germany	5-15-1965	8-12-1968
	Fort Benning Georgia	8-12-1968	2-21-1969
	Cam Ranh Bay Vietnam	6-30-1971	8-1-1972
4-17	7th Infantry Division	3-16-1985	8-15-1993

18th Infantry Regiment-Active Component

1-18	1st Infantry Division	2-15-1957	4-14-1959
	8th Infantry Division	4-14-1959	4-1-1963
	1st Infantry Division	4-1-1963	10-1-1983
	197th Infantry Brigade	6-16-1989	8-16-1991
	24th Infantry Division	8-16-1991	2-16-1996
	1st Infantry Division	2-16-1996	Present
2-18	1st Infantry Division	10-1-1963	4-15-1970
	197th Infantry Brigade	6-16-1989	8-16-1991
	24th Infantry Division	8-16-1991	2-16-1996
3-18	94th Infantry Division	5-1-1959	1-7-1963
	187th Infantry Brigade	1-7-1963	4-15-1994
4-18	Berlin Brigade	9-1-1963	9-13-1972
	3rd Armored Division	6-16-1989	12-16-1991
5-18	3rd Armored Division	6-16-1989	12-16-1991

19th Infantry Regiment-Active Component

1-19	24th Infantry Division		6-5-1958	4-15-1970
	25th Infantry Division		6-5-1972	7-16-1986
	Fort Benning Georgia	T	8-27-1987	5-18-2007
	198th Infantry Brigade	T	5-18-2007	Present
2-19	25th Infantry Division		2-1-1957	3-25-1958
	25th Infantry Division		7-1-1961	2-19-1962
	24th Infantry Division		2-1-1963	5-1-1966
	24th Infantry Division		5-21-1975	12-16-1987
	Fort Benning Georgia	T	4-1-1997	5-18-2007
	198th Infantry Brigade	T	5-18-2007	Present
3-19	24th Infantry Division		2-1-1963	4-15-1970
	24th Infantry Division		5-21-1975	8-25-1989
4-19	83rd Infantry Division		3-20-1959	4-15-1963
E-19	South Korea		2-1-1963	12-1-1967

20th Infantry Regiment-Active Component

1-20	Fort Kobbe Canal Zone	11-1-1957	8-8-1962
	11th Infantry Brigade	7-1-1966	2-15-1969
	23rd Infantry Division	2-15-1969	11-30-1971
2-20	6th Infantry Division	11-24-1967	7-25-1968
3-20	90th Infantry Division	4-1-1959	3-27-1963
	198th Infantry Brigade	5-10-1967	5-12-1967
	6th Infantry Division	11-24-1967	7-25-1968
4-20	193rd Infantry Brigade	8-8-1962	10-1-1983
E-20	South Korea	6-24-1960	1-1-1966
	1st Field Force Vietnam	9-25-1967	2-1-1969
5-20	2nd Infantry Division	8-16-1986	8-15-1995
	25th Infantry Division	8-16-1995	9-16-2000
	2nd Infantry Division	9-16-2000	Present
6-20	6th Infantry Division	11-24-1967	7-25-1968

21st Infantry Regiment-Active Component

1-21	24th Infantry Division	7-1-1958	4-15-1970
	25th Infantry Division	6-5-1972	Present
2-21	25th Infantry Division	2-1-1957	2-1-1963
	24th Infantry Division	2-1-1963	4-15-1970
	24th Infantry Division	6-21-1975	12-16-1987

3-21	63rd Infantry Division	5-1-1959	4-1-1963
	196th Infantry Brigade	9-15-1965	2-15-1969
	23rd Infantry Division	2-15-1969	11-1-1971
	196th Infantry Brigade	11-1-1971	8-23-1972
	25th Infantry Division	1-16-1986	7-15-1995
	25th Infantry Division	3-16-2000	6-1-2006
	25th Infantry Division	12-16-2006	Present
4-21	25th Infantry Division	12-6-1969	12-15-1970
	11th Infantry Brigade	11-1-1967	2-15-1969
	23rd Infantry Division	2-15-1969	11-1-1971
	7th Infantry Division	1-16-1986	9-15-1993
5-21	25th Infantry Division	12-6-1965	1-3-1966
E-21	197th Infantry Brigade		

22nd Infantry Regiment-Active Component

1-22	4th Infantry Division	4-1-1957	8-1-1984
	10th Infantry Division	5-1-1986	2-16-1996
	4th Infantry Division	2-16-1996	Present
2-22	4th Infantry Division	10-1-1963	8-1-1967
	25th Infantry Division	8-1-1967	12-15-1970
	4th Infantry Division	12-15-1970	8-1-1984
	10th Infantry Division	9-1-1986	Present
3-22	96th Infantry Division	6-1-1959	3-15-1963
	4th Infantry Division	11-1-1965	8-1-1967
	25th Infantry Division	8-1-1967	4-25-1971
	10th Infantry Division		
	25th Infantry Division	7-16-1986	7-16-1995
4-22	25th Infantry Division	11-16-1986	7-16-1995

23rd Infantry Regiment-Active Component

1-23	2nd Infantry Division	6-20-1957	12-16-1957
	Fort Richardson Alaska	12-16-1957	1-25-1963
	2nd Infantry Division	1-25-1963	12-16-1986
	2nd Infantry Division	4-16-1995	Present
2-23	2nd Infantry Division	6-14-1958	6-21-1971
	9th Infantry Division	1-21-1983	9-28-1990
	2nd Infantry Division	6-1-2006	Present
3-23	90th Infantry Division	4-1-1959	3-27-1963

	2nd Infantry Division		7-1-1965	4-2-1971
4-23	Fort Richardson Alaska		1-25-1963	5-20-1963
	172nd Infantry Brigade		5-20-1963	1-14-1966
	25th Infantry Division		1-14-1966	6-5-1972
	172nd Infantry Brigade		8-2-1972	1-6-1983
	9th Infantry Division		1-21-1983	9-28-1990
	172nd Infantry Brigade		3-16-2004	12-5-2006
	2nd Infantry Division		12-5-2006	Present
5-23	172nd Infantry Brigade		12-20-1965	12-15-1970
F-23	South Korea		9-24-1963	1-1-1966

24th Infantry Regiment-Active Component

1-24	25th Infantry Division		8-16-1995	6-1-2006
	25th Infantry Division		12-16-2006	Present

26th Infantry Regiment-Active Component

1-26	1st Infantry Division		2-15-1957	4-14-1959
	8th Infantry Division		4-14-1959	10-24-1962
	2nd Infantry Division		10-24-1962	2-15-1963
	1st Infantry Division		2-15-1963	2-23-1983
	Fort Dix New Jersey	T	4-3-1987	8-22-1990
	1st Infantry Division		4-9-1996	Present
2-26	1st Infantry Division		2-1-1963	1-14-1964
	Fort Dix New Jersey	T	4-3-1987	8-22-1990
	1st Infantry Division		4-17-2007	9-16-2007
3-26	77th Infantry Division		5-1-1959	3-26-1963
	198th Infantry Brigade		5-10-1967	5-12-1967
	Fort Dix New Jersey	T	4-3-1987	8-22-1990
4-26	Fort Dix New Jersey	T	4-3-1987	8-22-1990
5-26	Fort Dix New Jersey	T	4-3-1987	8-22-1990

27th Infantry Regiment-Active Component

1-27	25th Infantry Division	2-1-1957	Present
B-27	South Korea	6-24-1960	3-26-1963
2-27	25th Infantry Division	8-26-1963	6-5-1972
	7th Infantry Division	6-10-1987	9-15-1993
	25th Infantry Division	8-16-1995	Present

3-27	63rd Infantry Division		5-1-1959	12-31-1965
	25th Infantry Division		12-6-1969	12-15-1970
	7th Infantry Division		7-1-1987	9-15-1993
4-27	63rd Infantry Division		4-1-1963	12-31-1965
	25th Infantry Division		7-25-1987	8-15-1993

28th Infantry Regiment-Active Component

1-28	8th Infantry Division		8-1-1957	5-1-1959
	1st Infantry Division		5-1-1959	2-28-1983
	Fort Jackson South Carolina	T	2-27-1987	11-16-2005
	1st Infantry Division		1-16-2006	Present
2-28	1st Infantry Division		2-15-1957	12-26-1958
	24th Infantry Division		12-26-1958	2-1-1963
	1st Infantry Division		1-31-1964	4-15-1970
	8th Infantry Division		8-31-1973	8-1-1984
	Fort Jackson South Carolina	T	2-28-1987	9-30-1994
	Fort Jackson South Carolina	T	9-16-1996	11-16-2005
3-28	83rd Infantry Division		3-20-1959	12-31-1965
	1st Infantry Division		9-21-1976	12-16-1979
	4th Infantry Division		12-16-1979	8-1-1984
	Fort Jackson South Carolina	T	2-27-1987	9-1-1993

29th Infantry Regiment-Active Component

1-29	Fort Benning Georgia		7-25-1957	7-25-1958
	1st Infantry Brigade		7-25-1958	9-20-1962
	197th Infantry Brigade		9-20-1962	9-24-1962
	Fort Benning Georgia	T	3-21-1973	
	197th Infantry Brigade	T		Present
2-29	10th Infantry Division		7-1-1957	6-14-1958
	197th Infantry Brigade		2-1-1963	11-14-1965
	Fort Benning Georgia	T	2-27-1987	
	197th Infantry Brigade	T		Present
3-29	81st Infantry Division		5-1-1959	12-31-1965
4-29	197th Infantry Brigade		9-24-1962	1-4-1963
	Fort Benning Georgia		1-4-1963	2-1-1963
	81st Infantry Division		4-1-1963	12-31-1965

30th Infantry Regiment-Active Component

1-30	3rd Infantry Division		7-1-1957	6-16-1989
	3rd Infantry Division		8-16-1992	1-15-1994
	3rd Infantry Division		2-16-1996	Present
2-30	Fort Benning Georgia		1-22-1958	4-1-1963
	3rd Infantry Division		4-1-1963	6-16-1989
	10th Infantry Division		1-16-2005	Present
3-30	63rd Infantry Division		4-1-1963	12-31-1965
4-30	Fort Sill Oklahoma		4-1-1963	1-11-1972
	Fort Benning Georgia	T	2-27-1987	8-16-1992
E-30	Fort Rucker Alabama		8-26-1966	7-1-1978
F-30	Fort Riley Kansas		2-1-1967	3-25-1967

31st Infantry Regiment-Active Component

1-31	7th Infantry Division	7-1-1957	3-31-1971
	2nd Infantry Division	3-31-1971	12-16-1986
2-31	Fort Rucker Alabama	3-24-1958	7-1-1963
	7th Infantry Division	7-1-1963	3-31-1971
	7th Infantry Division	6-21-1975	4-29-1983
3-31	63rd Infantry Division	5-1-1959	12-31-1965
	7th Infantry Division	10-21-1975	
4-31	196th Infantry Brigade	9-15-1965	2-15-1969
	23rd Infantry Division	2-15-1969	11-30-1971
	196th Infantry Brigade	11-30-1971	6-29-1972
	Fort Sill Oklahoma	6-29-1972	6-15-1995
	10th Infantry Division	2-16-1996	Present
5-31	Fort Rucker Alabama	7-1-1963	6-23-1967
	197th Infantry Brigade	6-23-1967	3-21-1973
6-31	Fort Lewis Washington	11-1-1967	2-15-1969
	9th Infantry Division	2-15-1969	10-13-1970
	7th Infantry Division	11-21-1975	10-1-1981
	Fort Irwin California	10-1-1981	1-16-1988

32nd Infantry Regiment-Active Component

1-32	7th Infantry Division	7-1-1957	3-31-1971
	2nd Infantry Division	3-31-1971	10-21-1978
	7th Infantry Division	8-7-1980	6-10-1987

14

	10th Infantry Division		2-16-1996	Present
2-32	7th Infantry Division		7-1-1963	3-31-1971
	7th Infantry Division		5-21-1975	1-16-1986
C-32	Fort Bragg North Carolina		6-25-1958	2-7-1963
3-32	7th Infantry Division		7-1-1963	3-31-1971
	2nd Infantry Division		3-31-1971	6-21-1971
	7th Infantry Division		6-21-1971	1-16-1986
	Fort Benning Georgia	T	8-28-1987	
4-32	81st Infantry Division		5-1-1959	4-1-1963

34th Infantry Regiment-Active Component

1-34	24th Infantry Division		6-5-1958	4-15-1970
	Fort Jackson South Carolina	T	2-27-1987	1-15-1993
	Fort Jackson South Carolina	T	1-12-1996	1-26-2007
	165th Infantry Brigade	T	1-26-2007	Present
2-34	7th Infantry Division		7-1-1957	2-1-1963
	24th Infantry Division		2-1-1963	4-15-1970
	24th Infantry Division		6-21-1975	12-16-1987
	Fort Jackson South Carolina	T	2-27-1987	1-15-1993
3-34	79th Infantry Division		3-23-1959	3-28-1963
	24th Infantry Division		9-21-1975	1-23-1976
	Fort Jackson South Carolina	T	2-27-1987	3-31-1989
	Fort Jackson South Carolina	T	10-1-2005	1-26-2007
	165th Infantry Brigade	T	1-26-2007	Present

35th Infantry Regiment-Active Component

1-35	25th Infantry Division		2-1-1957	8-1-1967
	4th Infantry Division		8-1-1967	4-10-1970
	25th Infantry Division		12-15-1970	7-27-1987
2-35	25th Infantry Division		2-19-1962	8-1-1967
	4th Infantry Division		8-1-1967	12-15-1970
	25th Infantry Division		12-15-1970	4-25-1971
	25th Infantry Division		8-16-1995	Present
3-35	94th Infantry Division		5-1-1959	1-7-1963
	187th Infantry Brigade		1-7-1963	4-15-1994

36th Infantry Regiment-Active Component

1-36	1st Armored Division		2-15-1957	12-23-1957
	3rd Armored Division		2-3-1962	6-16-1989
	1st Armored Division		2-16-1996	Present
2-36	3rd Armored Division		10-1-1957	10-16-1988
3-36	3rd Armored Division		2-3-1962	10-16-1988
	1st Armored Division			Present
4-36	Fort Benning Georgia	T	2-27-1987	

38th Infantry Regiment-Active Component

1-39	Fort Benning Georgia		11-8-1957	3-4-1958
	2nd Infantry Division		2-19-1962	12-16-1986
	Fort Benning Georgia	T	8-28-1987	4-27-2006
	2nd Infantry Division		6-1-2006	Present
2-38	3rd Infantry Division		7-1-1957	4-1-1963
	2nd Infantry Division		4-1-1963	4-2-1971
3-38	96th Infantry Division		6-1-1959	3-15-1963
	191st Infantry Brigade		3-15-1963	2-28-1968

39th Infantry Regiment-Active Component

1-39	9th Infantry Division		12-1-1957	1-31-1962
	197th Infantry Brigade		9-24-1962	1-4-1963
	8th Infantry Division		4-1-1963	8-1-1984
2-39	4th Infantry Division		4-1-1957	10-1-1963
	9th Infantry Division		2-1-1966	9-25-1969
	9th Infantry Division		4-21-1972	1-21-1983
	Fort Dix New Jersey	T	4-3-1987	8-22-1990
	Fort Jackson South Carolina	T	8-22-1990	1-26-2007
	165th Infantry Brigade	T	1-26-2007	Present
3-39	9th Infantry Division		2-1-1966	9-25-1969
	9th Infantry Division		7-21-1972	1-21-1983
	Fort Dix New Jersey	T	4-3-1987	8-22-1990
4-39	9th Infantry Division		2-1-1966	9-25-1969
	Fort Dix New Jersey	T	4-3-1987	8-22-1990

41st Infantry-Active Component

1-41	2nd Armored Division		7-1-1957	6-15-1992
	2nd Armored Division		12-16-1992	12-15-1995
	1st Armored Division		2-16-1997	Present
2-41	4th Armored Division		4-1-1957	7-1-1963
	2nd Armored Division		7-1-1963	6-15-1992
3-41	Fort Ord California		4-25-1961	12-31-1962
	2nd Armored Division		10-1-1983	3-16-1991
	1st Cavalry Division		3-16-1991	11-29-1992
	2nd Armored Division		11-29-1992	12-15-1995
4-41	194th Armored Brigade		12-21-1962	1-4-1968
	2nd Armored Division		10-1-1983	6-15-1992
D-41	Fort Ord California		1-4-1968	3-20-1970
E-41	Fort Ord California		1-4-1968	3-20-1970
F-41	Fort Ord California		1-4-1968	3-20-1970
G-41	Fort Ord California		1-4-1968	3-20-1970
H-41	Fort Ord California		1-4-1968	3-20-1970

46th Infantry Regiment-Active Component

1-46	1st Armored Division		2-15-1957	12-23-1957
	Germany		4-1-1958	2-3-1962
	1st Armored Division		2-3-1962	5-12-1967
	198th Infantry Brigade		5-12-1967	2-15-1969
	23rd Infantry Division		2-15-1969	11-1-1971
	196th Infantry Brigade		11-1-1971	9-13-1972
	1st Armored Division		9-13-1972	8-1-1984
	Fort Knox Kentucky	T	1-30-1987	7-10-2007
	194th Armored Brigade	T	7-10-2007	Present
2-46	3rd Armored Division		10-1-1957	2-3-1962
	1st Armored Division		2-3-1962	9-13-1972
	Fort Knox Kentucky	T	1-30-1987	7-10-2007
	194th Armored Brigade	T	7-10-2007	Present
3-46	Germany		2-1-1962	2-1-1963
	Fort Knox Kentucky	T	1-301987	
4-46	1st Armored Division		5-12-1967	5-5-1971
	Fort Knox Kentucky	T	1-30-1987	
5-46	Fort Hood Texas		10-2-1968	3-31-1968
	198th Infantry Brigade		3-31-1968	2-15-1969
	23rd Infantry Division		2-15-1969	5-22-1971
	Fort Knox Kentucky	T	10-1-2000	2-16-2002

47th Infantry Regiment-Active Component

1-47	9th Infantry Division		12-1-1957	1-31-1962
	171st Infantry Brigade		7-1-1963	11-13-1972
2-47	4th Infantry Division		4-1-1957	10-1-1963
	9th Infantry Division		2-1-1966	10-13-1970
	9th Infantry Division		10-21-1972	8-15-1988
	Fort Leonard Wood Missouri	T	4-15-1996	2-1-1999
	Fort Benning Georgia	T	3-1-1999	1-26-2007
	192nd Infantry Brigade		1-26-2007	Present
3-47	81st Infantry Division		5-1-1959	4-1-1963
	9th Infantry Division		2-1-1969	10-13-1970
	9th Infantry Division		3-21-1973	2-16-1991
	199th Infantry Brigade		2-16-1991	1-14-1994
	Fort Leonard Wood Missouri	T	10-2-1996	2-1-1999
	Fort Benning Georgia	T	3-1-1999	12-15-2003
	Fort Benning Georgia	T	4-27-2006	1-26-2007
	192nd Infantry Brigade		1-26-2007	Present
4-47	9th Infantry Division		2-1-1966	8-1-1969

48th Infantry Regiment-Active Component

1-48	1st Armored Division		2-15-1957	12-23-1957
	Germany		4-1-1958	7-1-1963
	3rd Armored Division		7-1-1963	6-16-1989
	Fort Leonard Wood Missouri	T	4-15-1996	1-31-2007
	187th Infantry Brigade	T	1-31-2007	5-17-2007
	3rd Chemical Brigade	T	5-17-2007	Present
2-48	3rd Armored Division		7-1-1957	10-16-1983

50th Infantry Regiment-Active Component

1-50	2nd Armored Division		7-1-1957	9-1-1967
	South Vietnam		9-1-1967	12-16-1970
	2nd Armored Division		12-16-1970	10-1-1983
	Fort Benning Georgia	T	8-28-1987	5-18-2007
	198th Infantry Brigade	T	5-18-2007	Present
2-50	4th Armored Division		4-1-1957	7-1-1963
	2nd Armored Division		7-1-1963	10-1-1983
3-50	Germany		4-1-1958	7-15-1963

E-50	9th Infantry Division	12-20-1967	2-1-1969
F-50	South Vietnam	12-20-1967	2-1-1969
	South Vietnam	6-30-1971	11-16-1972

51st Infantry Regiment-Active Component

1-51	1st Armored Division	7-1-1957	7-1-1963
	4th Armored Division	7-1-1963	5-10-1971
	1st Armored Division	5-10-1971	6-16-1984
2-51	4th Armored Division	7-1-1957	5-10-1971
	1st Armored Division	5-10-1971	4-20-1974
3-51	Germany	4-1-1958	4-1-1963
	4th Armored Division	4-1-1963	5-10-1971
D-51	Fort Lewis Washington	6-1-1966	11-29-1966
	South Vietnam	11-29-1966	6-30-1972
E-51	23rd Infantry Division	12-20-1967	2-1-1969
	South Vietnam	2-1-1969	7-21-1969
	5th Corps Germany	9-16-1986	Present
F-51	199th Infantry Brigade	9-25-1967	2-1-1969
	South Vietnam	2-1-1969	12-28-1969
	7th Corps Germany	9-16-1986	
	18th Corps Fort Bragg N. Carolina		Present

52nd Infantry Regiment-Active Component

1-52	Fort Hood Texas	3-1-1957	2-3-1962
	1st Armored Division	2-3-1962	5-12-1967
	198th Infantry Brigade	5-12-1967	2-15-1969
	23rd Infantry Division	2-15-1969	11-30-1971
	1st Armored Division	9-15-1972	11-16-1987
	Fort Irwin California	1-16-1988	10-16-1991
	177th Armored Brigade	10-16-1991	10-15-1994
A-52	172nd Infantry Brigade	1-16-2004	11-16-2006
	2nd Infantry Division	11-16-2006	Present
2-52	3rd Armored Division	10-1-1957	2-3-1962
	1st Armored Division	2-3-1962	9-10-1963
	1st Armored Division	5-12-1967	11-30-1971
B-52	25th Infantry Division	11-16-2005	Present
C-52	Fort Lewis Washington	6-1-1966	12-1-1966
	South Vietnam	12-1-1966	8-15-1972

	2nd Infantry Division		9-16-2000	Present
D-52	Fort Lewis Washington		6-1-1966	12-1-1966
	South Vietnam		12-1-1966	11-22-1969
	South Vietnam		6-30-1971	11-26-1972
	25th Infantry Division		7-16-2002	6-1-2006
	25th Infantry Division		12-16-2006	Present
E-52	1st Cavalry Division		12-20-1967	2-1-1969
	3rd Corps Fort Hood Texas		11-16-1995	Present
F-52	1st Infantry Division		12-20-1967	2-1-1969
	1st Corps Fort Lewis Washington		6-16-1996	9-15-1997
	2nd Infantry Division		6-1-2006	Present

54th Infantry Regiment-Active Component

1-54	4th Armored Division		4-1-1957	5-10-1971
	1st Armored Division		5-10-1971	
2-54	Fort Knox Kentucky		9-23-1957	7-15-1963
	4th Armored Division		7-15-1963	5-10-1971
	Fort Benning Georgia	T	8-28-1987	1-26-2007
	192nd Infantry Brigade	T	1-26-2007	Present
C-54	Fort Lewis Washington		6-1-1966	11-29-1966
	South Vietnam		11-29-1966	4-30-1972
4-54	Fort Knox Kentucky		7-1-1963	4-15-1968
	194th Armored Brigade		4-15-1968	
E-54	Fort Stewart Georgia		7-25-1968	6-30-1971

58th Infantry Regiment-Active Component

1-58	1st Infantry Brigade		5-16-1960	9-20-1962
	197th Infantry Brigade		9-20-1962	6-16-1987
2-58	2nd Armored Division		7-1-1957	7-1-1963
	2nd Armored Division		4-1-1975	5-31-1981
	Fort Benning Georgia	T	8-28-1987	5-18-2007
	198th Infantry Brigade	T	5-18-2007	Present
C-58	194th Armored Brigade		12-2-1963	5-15-1964
	Nelligan Germany		5-15-1965	8-7-1968
	Fort Riley Kansas		8-7-1968	1-19-1969
	Fort Carson Colorado		1-19-1969	2-10-1969
D-58	Fort Lewis Washington		6-1-1966	11-22-1966
	South Vietnam		11-22-1966	6-22-1972
E-58	4th Infantry Division		12-20-1967	2-1-1969
F-58	101st Airborne Division		1-10-1968	2-1-1968

59th Infantry Regiment-Army Reserve

| 1-59 | 96th Infantry Division | | 5-20-1959 | 3-15-1963 |
| | 191st Infantry Brigade | | 3-15-1963 | 2-28-1968 |

60th Infantry Regiment-Active Component

1-60	9th Infantry Division		12-1-1957	1-31-1962
	172nd Infantry Brigade		7-1-1963	1-21-1983
2-60	2nd Infantry Brigade		2-15-1958	2-19-1962
	9th Infantry Division		2-1-1966	10-13-1970
	9th Infantry Division		10-21-1972	2-15-1991
	Fort Jackson South Carolina	T	4-15-1996	1-31-2007
	193rd Infantry Brigade	T	1-31-2007	Present
3-60	9th Infantry Division		2-1-1966	8-1-1969
	9th Infantry Division		11-21-1972	8-15-1988
	Fort Jackson South Carolina	T	11-16-2005	1-31-2007
	193rd Infantry Brigade	T	1-31-2007	Present
5-60	9th Infantry Division		2-1-1966	10-13-1970
E-60	9th Infantry Division		7- -1982	- -1984

61st Infantry Regiment-Active Component

1-61	5th Infantry Division		2-19-1962	8-2-1971
	4th Infantry Division		8-2-1971	8-24-1974
	5th Infantry Division		8-24-1974	11-16-1987
	Fort Jackson South Carolina	T	6-13-1993	1-26-2007
	165th Infantry Brigade	T	1-26-2007	Present
2-61	5th Infantry Division		2-19-1962	12-15-1970
	4th Infantry Division		12-15-1970	8-2-1971
	Fort Jackson South Carolina	T	2-27-1987	6-13-1993
3-61	5th Infantry Division		11-15-1969	12-15-1970

65th Infantry Regiment-National Guard

1-65	92nd Infantry Brigade		2-15-1959	
	29th Infantry Division			
E-65	Puerto Rico		4-1-1971	2-29-1980

69th Infantry Regiment-National Guard

1-69	42nd Infantry Division	4-15-1963	9-1-1993
	42nd Infantry Division	9-1-1996	Present
2-69	42nd Infantry Division	4-15-1963	4-1-1975

71st Infantry Regiment-National Guard

1-71	42nd Infantry Division	3-16-1959	9-1-1992

72nd Infantry Regiment-National Guard

A-72	Jericho Vermont	9-1-1982	4-1-1983

75th Ranger Regiment-Active Component

A-75	Fort Benning Georgia	2-21-1969	10-1-1969
	1st Cavalry Division	2-9-1970	12-19-1974
B-75	Fort Carson Colorado	2-10-1969	11-1-1974
C-75	1st Field Force Vietnam	2-1-1969	10-25-1971
D-75	2nd Field Force Vietnam	2-10-1969	4-10-1971
E-75	9th Infantry Division	2-1-1969	8-23-1969
	9th Infantry Division	10-1-1969	10-12-1970
F-75	25th Infantry Division	2-1-1969	3-15-1970
G-75	23rd Infantry Division	2-1-1969	10-1-1971
H-75	1st Cavalry Division	2-1-1969	8-15-1972
I-75	1st Infantry Division	2-1-1969	4-7-1970
K-75	4th Infantry Division	2-1-1969	12-10-1970
L-75	101st Airborne Division	2-1-1969	12-26-1970
M-75	199th Infantry Brigade	2-1-1969	10-12-1970
N-75	173rd Airborne Brigade	2-1-1969	8-27-1971
O-75	82nd Airborne Division	2-1-1969	11-20-1969
	Fort Richardson Alaska	8-4-1970	9-29-1972
P-75	5th Infantry Division	2-1-1969	8-31-1971
1-75	Fort Stewart Georgia	1-31-1974	Present
2-75	Fort Lewis Washington	10-1-1974	Present
3-75	Fort Benning Georgia	10-3-1984	Present
4-TB	Camp Daily Georgia	- -1984	Present
5-TB	Camp Merrill Georgia	- -1984	Present
6-TB	Camp Rudder Florida	- -1984	Present
7-TB	Fort Bliss Texas	- -1984	Present

22

87th Infantry Regiment-Active Component

1-87	10th Infantry Division		7-1-1957	6-14-1958
	2nd Infantry Division		6-14-1958	9-4-1963
	8th Infantry Division		9-4-1963	8-1-1984
	10th Infantry Division		5-22-1987	Present
2-87	2nd Infantry Division		2-15-1963	9-4-1963
	8th Infantry Division		9-4-1963	5-1-1966
	8th Infantry Division		8-31-1973	6-16-1986
	10th Infantry Division		6-27-1988	Present
C-87	Fort Lewis Washington		6-1-1966	11-29-1966
	South Vietnam		11-29-1966	11-26-1972
3-87	Fort Carson Colorado	AR	7-1-1975	
D-87	Fort Lewis Washington		6-1-1966	12-1-1966
	South Vietnam		12-1-1966	11-8-1969
	South Vietnam		6-30-1971	4-30-1972
4-87	25th Infantry Division		7-16-1987	8-16-1995
5-87	193rd Infantry Brigade		5-1-1987	10-15-1994
	Panama		10-15-1994	10-15-1995

101st Infantry Regiment-National Guard

1-101	26th Infantry Division	5-1-1959	9-1-1993

102nd Infantry Regiment-National Guard

1-102	43rd Infantry Division	5-1-1959	5-1-1963
	Connecticut	5-1-1963	12-16-1967
	26th Infantry Division	12-16-1967	9-1-1993
	43rd Infantry Brigade	9-1-1993	10-1-1995
	29th Infantry Division	10-1-1995	
	42nd Infantry Division		
2-102	43rd Infantry Division	5-1-1959	5-1-1963
	Connecticut	5-1-1963	12-16-1967
	26th Infantry Division	12-16-1967	9-1-992
3-102	26th Infantry Division	4-15-1992	9-1-1992

104th Infantry Regiment-National Guard

1-104	26th Infantry Division	5-1-1959	9-1-1993
	26th Infantry Brigade	9-1-1993	10-1-1995
	29th Infantry Division	10-1-1995	
2-104	26th Infantry Division	4-1-1963	9-1-1993

105th Infantry Regiment-National Guard

Unit	Assignment	From	To
1-105	27th Armored Division	3-16-1959	2-1-1968
	42nd Infantry Division	2-1-1968	4-1-1986
	27th Infantry Brigade	4-1-1986	
2-105	42nd Infantry Division	4-1-1986	9-1-1993

106th Infantry Regiment-National Guard

Unit	Assignment	From	To
1-106	42nd Infantry Division	3-16-1959	4-1-1986
2-106	Brooklyn New York	3-1-1964	2-1-1968
	42nd Infantry Division	2-1-1968	12-1-1971

107th Infantry Regiment-National Guard

Unit	Assignment	From	To
1-107	42nd Infantry Division	3-16-1959	9-1-1993
2-107	42nd Infantry Division	4-15-1963	2-1-1968

108th Infantry Regiment-National Guard

Unit	Assignment	From	To
1-108	27th Armored Division	3-16-1959	2-1-1968
	50th Armored Division	2-1-1968	4-1-1975
	42nd Infantry Division	4-1-1975	9-1-1996
	27th Infantry Brigade	9-1-1996	
2-108	27th Armored Division	3-16-1959	2-1-1968
	42nd Infantry Division	2-1-1968	4-1-1986
	27th Infantry Brigade	4-1-1986	
	42nd Infantry Division		
3-108	27th Infantry Brigade	4-1-1986	9-1-1996

109th Infantry Regiment-National Guard

Unit	Assignment	From	To
1-109	28th Infantry Division	6-1-1959	Present
2-109	28th Infantry Division	4-1-1963	9-1-1991
3-109	Milton Pennsylvania	3-24-1964	2-17-1968
	28th Infantry Division	4-1-1975	10-1-1994

110th Infantry Regiment-National Guard

Unit	Assignment	From	To
1-110	28th Infantry Division	6-1-1959	2-17-1968
	42nd Infantry Division	2-17-1968	4-1-1975
	28th Infantry Division	4-1-1975	Present
2-110	28th Infantry Division	4-1-1975	9-1-1995

111th Infantry Regiment-National Guard

1-111	28th Infantry Division	6-1-1959	Present
2-111	28th Infantry Division	6-1-1959	2-17-1968
	42nd Infantry Division	2-17-1968	4-1-1975
	28th Infantry Division	4-1-1975	9-1-1995

112th Infantry Regiment-National Guard

1-112	28th Infantry Division	6-1-1959	2-17-1968
	42nd Infantry Division	2-17-1968	4-1-1975
	28th Infantry Division	4-1-1975	Present
2-112	28th Infantry Division	4-1-1975	Present
D-112	28th Infantry Division		Present

113th Infantry Regiment-National Guard

1-113	50th Armored Division	3-1-1959	9-1-1989
2-113	50th Armored Division	3-1-1959	9-1-1993
	42nd Infantry Division	9-1-1993	Present
3-113	50th Armored Division	6-1-1975	9-1-1991

114th Infantry Regiment-National Guard

1-114	50th Armored Division	3-1-1959	9-1-1993
	42nd Infantry Division	9-1-1993	Present
2-114	50th Armored Division	3-1-1959	2-1-1968
	50th Armored Division	7-1-1975	9-1-1991

115th Infantry Regiment-National Guard

1-115	29th Infantry Division	3-1-1959	2-1-1968
	28th Infantry Division	2-1-1968	4-1-1975
	58th Infantry Brigade	4-1-1975	7-1-1986
	29th Infantry Division	7-1-1986	9-3-2006
2-115	29th Infantry Division	3-1-1959	2-1-1968
	29th Infantry Division	7-1-1986	6-1-2003
D-115	29th Infantry Division (LAT)	6-1-2003	8-31-2006
E-115	29th Infantry Division (LAT)	6-1-2003	8-31-2006
F-115	29th Infantry Division (LAT)	6-1-2003	8-31-2006

116th Infantry Regiment-National Guard

1-116	29th Infantry Division	6-1-1959	2-1-1968
	28th Infantry Division	2-1-1968	4-1-1975
	116th Infantry Brigade	4-1-1975	6-1-1986
	29th Infantry Division	6-1-1986	Present
2-116	29th Infantry Division	6-1-1959	2-1-1968
	28th Infantry Division	2-1-1968	4-1-1975
	116th Infantry Brigade	4-1-1975	6-1-1986
	29th Infantry Division	6-1-1986	
3-116	28th Infantry Division	2-1-1968	4-1-1975
	116th Infantry Brigade	4-1-1975	6-1-1986
	29th Infantry Division	6-1-1986	Present

117th Infantry Regiment-National Guard

1-117	30th Armored Division	3-1-1959	11-1-1973
2-117	30th Armored Division	3-1-1959	11-1-1973
	278th Infantry Brigade	11-1-1973	5-1-1977
3-117	30th Armored Division	3-1-1959	1-1-1968
	Tennessee	1-1-1968	11-1-1973
	278th Infantry Brigade	11-1-1973	5-1-1977
	Tennessee	5-1-1977	2-1-1980
4-117	30th Armored Division	3-1-1959	11-1-1973
	30th Armored Brigade	11-1-1973	9-1-1996
	38th Infantry Division		

118th Infantry Regiment-National Guard

1-118	51st Infantry Division	4-1-1959	4-1-1963
	Mount Pleasant South Carolina	4-1-1963	1-1-1968
	30th Infantry Division	1-1-1968	11-30-1973
	218th Infantry Brigade	11-30-1973	
	35th Infantry Division		
2-118	51st Infantry Division	4-1-1959	4-1-1963
	Walterboro South Carolina	4-1-1963	1-1-1968
3-118	51st Infantry Division	4-1-1959	4-1-1963
	Florence South Carolina	4-1-1963	1-1-1968
4-118	Union South Carolina	4-1-1963	1-1-1968
	30th Infantry Division	1-1-1968	11-30-1973
	218th Infantry Brigade	11-30-1973	

119th Infantry Regiment-National Guard

1-119	30th Infantry Division	4-1-1959	3-10-1963
	30th Infantry Division	1-1-1968	11-30-1973
	30th Infantry Brigade	11-30-1973	9-1-2002
2-119	30th Infantry Division	4-1-1959	3-10-1963
4-119	30th Infantry Division	3-10-1963	1-1-1968
5-119	30th Infantry Division	3-10-1963	1-1-1968
6-119	30th Infantry Division	3-10-1963	1-1-1968

120th Infantry Regiment-National Guard

1-120	30th Infantry Division	4-1-1959	11-30-1973
	30th Infantry Brigade	11-30-1973	9-1-2002
	30th Armored Brigade	9-1-2002	
	29th Infantry Division		
2-120	30th Infantry Division	4-1-1959	1-1-1968
	North Carolina	1-1-1968	9-1-1992
3-120	30th Infantry Division	4-1-1959	1-1-1968

121st Infantry Regiment-National Guard

1-121	48th Armored Division	7-1-1959	1-1-1968
	30th Infantry Division	1-1-1968	11-30-1973
	48th Infantry Brigade	11-30-1973	
	35th Infantry Division		
2-121	48th Armored Division	7-1-1959	1-1-1968
	30th Infantry Division	1-1-1968	11-30-1973
	48th Infantry Brigade	11-30-1973	
	35th Infantry Division		
3-121	48th Armored Division	4-1-1963	1-1-1968
4-121	48th Armored Division	4-1-1963	1-1-1968
H-121	Newnan Georgia	9-1-1993	Present

122nd Infantry Regiment-National Guard

1-122	Winder Georgia	10-1-1980	9-1-1993

123rd Infantry Regiment-National Guard

1-123	47th Infantry Division	2-1-1968	2-10-1991
	34th Infantry Division	2-10-1991	9-1-1997
	35th Infantry Division	9-1-1997	10-1-1999

124th Infantry Regiment-National Guard

1-124	48th Armored Division	4-1-1959	4-1-1963
	St. Petersburg Florida	4-1-1963	1-1-1968
	53rd Infantry Brigade	1-1-1968	
	28th Infantry Division		
2-124	48th Armored Division	4-1-1959	4-1-1963
	53rd Armored Brigade	4-1-1963	1-1-1968
	53rd Infantry Brigade	1-1-1968	
	28th Infantry Division		
3-124	53rd Infantry Brigade	1-1-1968	

125th Infantry Regiment-National Guard

1-125	46th Infantry Division	3-15-1959	2-1-1968
	38th Infantry Division	2-1-1968	Present
2-125	46th Infantry Division	3-15-1959	2-1-1968

126th Infantry Regiment-National Guard

1-126	46th Infantry Division	3-15-1959	2-1-1968
2-126	46th Infantry Division	3-15-1959	2-1-1968
3-126	46th Infantry Division	3-15-1959	2-1-1968
	38th Infantry Division	2-1-1968	10-1-2000

127th Infantry Regiment-National Guard

1-127	32nd Infantry Division	2-15-1959	12-30-1967
	32nd Infantry Brigade	12-30-1967	4-1-1971
	Green Bay Wisconsin	4-1-1971	2-1-1980
2-127	32nd Infantry Division	2-15-1959	12-30-1967
	32nd Infantry Brigade	12-30-1967	9-1-1997
	34th Infantry Division	9-1-1997	9-1-2001
	32nd Infantry Brigade	9-1-2001	
	34th Infantry Division		
3-127	32nd Infantry Division	2-15-1959	12-30-1967

28

128th Infantry Regiment-National Guard

1-128	32nd Infantry Division	2-15-1959	12-30-1967
	32nd Infantry Brigade	12-30-1967	9-1-1997
	34th Infantry Division	9-1-1997	9-1-2001
	32nd Infantry Brigade	9-1-2001	
	34th Infantry Division		
2-128	32nd Infantry Division	2-15-1959	12-30-1967
	Elkhorn Wisconsin	12-30-1967	9-1-1993
	32nd Infantry Brigade	9-1-2001	
3-128	32nd Infantry Division	4-1-1963	12-30-1967

129th Infantry Regiment-National Guard

1-129	33rd Infantry Division	3-1-1959	2-1-1968
2-129	33rd Infantry Division	3-1-1959	2-1-1968
	33rd Infantry Brigade	2-1-1968	9-1-1995

130th Infantry Regiment-National Guard

1-130	33rd Infantry Division	3-1-1959	2-1-1968
2-130	33rd Infantry Division	3-1-1959	2-1-1968
	47th Infantry Division	2-1-1968	2-10-1991
	34th Infantry Division	2-10-1991	9-1-1997
	35th Infantry Division	9-1-1997	Present
3-130	33rd Infantry Division	3-1-1959	2-1-1968
	47th Infantry Division	2-1-1968	2-10-1991
	34th Infantry Division	2-10-1991	9-1-1995

131st Infantry Regiment-National Guard

1-131	33rd Infantry Division	3-1-1959	2-1-1968
	33rd Infantry Brigade	2-1-1968	9-1-1995
	34th Infantry Division	9-1-1995	9-1-1997
	35th Infantry Division	9-1-1997	

133rd Infantry Regiment-National Guard

1-133	34th Infantry Division	6-1-1959	4-1-1963
	Waterloo Iowa	4-1-1963	2-1-1968

	47th Infantry Division	2-1-1968	2-10-1991
	34th Infantry Division	2-10-1991	Present
2-133	34th Infantry Division	6-1-1959	4-1-1963
	67th Infantry Brigade	4-1-1963	2-1-1968
	47th Infantry Division	2-1-1968	2-10-1991
	34th Infantry Division	2-10-1991	9-1-1997
3-133	Dubuque Iowa	3-1-1964	2-1-1968

134th Infantry Regiment-National Guard

1-134	34th Infantry Division	5-1-1959	4-1-1963
	67th Infantry Brigade	4-1-1963	10-1-1985
	35th Infantry Division	10-1-1985	10-1-1999
2-134	34th Infantry Division	5-1-1959	4-1-1963
	67th Infantry Brigade	4-1-1963	10-1-1985
	35th Infantry Division	10-1-1985	10-1-1998

135th Infantry Regiment-National Guard

1-135	47th Infantry Division	2-22-1959	2-10-1991
	34th Infantry Division	2-10-1991	9-1-1992
2-135	47th Infantry Division	2-22-1959	2-10-1991
	34th Infantry Division	2-10-1991	Present
3-135	47th Infantry Division	4-1-1963	2-1-1968
4-135	47th Infantry Division	4-1-1963	2-1-1968

136th Infantry Regiment-National Guard

1-136	47th Infantry Division	2-22-1959	2-1-1968
	Minnesota	2-1-1968	1-1-1972
	47th Infantry Division	1-1-1972	2-10-1991
	34th Infantry Division	2-10-1991	9-1-1992
2-136	47th Infantry Division	2-22-1959	1-1-1972
	Minnesota	1-1-1972	10-1-1998
	34th Infantry Division	10-1-1998	Present
3-136	47th Infantry Division	2-22-1959	4-1-1963

137th Infantry Regiment-National Guard

1-137	35th Infantry Division	5-1-1959	4-1-1963
	69th Infantry Brigade	4-1-1963	10-1-1985
	35th Infantry Division	10-1-1985	9-1-1993

30

2-137	35th Infantry Division	5-1-1959	4-1-1963
	69th Infantry Brigade	4-1-1963	10-1-1985
	35th Infantry Division	10-1-1985	Present
3-137	69th Infantry Brigade	5-13-1969	2-1-1976

138th Infantry Regiment-National Guard

1-138	35th Infantry Division	4-15-1959	4-1-1963
	69th Infantry Brigade	4-1-1963	2-1-1968
	Missouri	2-1-1968	5-1-1974

140th Infantry Regiment-National Guard

1-140	35th Infantry Division	4-15-1959	4-1-1963
	Cape Girardeau Missouri	4-1-1963	2-1-1968
2-140	35th Infantry Division	4-15-1959	4-1-1963
	Popular Bluff Missouri	4-1-1963	2-1-1968

141st Infantry Regiment-National Guard

1-141	36th Infantry Division	3-16-1959	11-1-1965
	36th Infantry Brigade	11-1-1965	11-1-1973
	49th Armored Division	11-1-1973	5-1-2004
	36th Infantry Division	5-1-2004	Present
2-141	36th Infantry Division	3-1-1963	11-1-1965
	36th Infantry Brigade	11-1-1965	11-1-1973
	49th Armored Division	11-1-1973	9-1-1995
3-141	36th Infantry Division	1-15-1968	11-1-1973
	49th Armored Division	11-1-1973	9-1-1984
	McClellan Texas	9-1-1984	9-1-1995
	49th Armored Division	9-1-1995	5-1-2004
	36th Infantry Division	5-1-2004	Present

142nd Infantry Regiment-National Guard

1-142	36th Infantry Division	3-16-1959	1-15-1968
2-142	36th Infantry Division	3-16-1959	1-15-1968
	72nd Infantry Brigade	1-15-1968	11-1-1973
	49th Armored Division	11-1-1973	5-1-2004
	36th Infantry Division	5-1-2004	Present

143rd Infantry Regiment-National Guard

1-143	36th Infantry Division	3-16-1959	3-1-1963
	71st Airborne Brigade	1-15-1968	11-1-1973
	36th Airborne Brigade	11-1-1973	4-1-1980
2-143	36th Infantry Division	3-1-1963	1-15-1968
	71st Airborne Brigade	1-15-1968	11-1-1973
	36th Airborne Brigade	11-1-1973	4-1-1980
3-143	36th Infantry Division	3-1-1963	11-1-1965
	36th Infantry Brigade	11-1-1965	1-15-1968
	71st Airborne Brigade	1-15-1968	11-1-1973
G-143	Houston Texas	4-1-1980	

144th Infantry Regiment-National Guard

1-144	49th Armored Division	3-16-1959	1-15-1968
2-144	49th Armored Division	3-16-1959	1-15-1968
3-144	49th Armored Division	3-16-1959	1-15-1968
	72nd Infantry Brigade	1-15-1968	11-1-1973
	49th Armored Division	11-1-1973	5-1-2004
	36th Infantry Division	3-16-1959	1-15-1968

145th Infantry Regiment-National Guard

1-145	37th Infantry Division	9-1-1959	2-15-1968
	Ohio	2-15-1968	9-30-1974
2-145	Wooster Ohio	9-1-1959	2-15-1968
	38th Infantry Division	2-15-1968	5-1-1968
3-145	37th Infantry Division	4-1-1963	2-15-1968

147th Infantry Regiment-National Guard

1-147	37th Infantry Division	9-1-1959	2-15-1968
	38th Infantry Division	2-15-1968	3-1-1977
	73rd Infantry Brigade	3-1-1977	9-1-1992
	37th Infantry Brigade	9-1-1992	9-1-1993
	28th Infantry Division	9-1-1993	9-1-1994
2-147	37th Infantry Division	9-1-1959	2-15-1968

148th Infantry Regiment-National Guard

1-148	37th Infantry Division	9-1-1959	4-1-1963
	Ohio	4-1-1963	11-1-1965
	37th Infantry Division	11-1-1965	2-15-1968
	38th Infantry Division	2-15-1968	3-1-1977
	73rd Infantry Brigade	3-1-1977	9-1-1992
	37th Infantry Brigade	9-1-1992	9-1-1993
	28th Infantry Division	9-1-1993	9-1-1994
	38th Infantry Division	9-1-1994	Present
2-148	37th Infantry Division	9-1-1959	2-15-1968

149th Infantry Regiment-National Guard

1-149	Barbourville Kentucky	4-6-1959	2-1-1968
	Barbourville Kentucky	11-1-1974	11-1-1980
	149th Armored Brigade	11-1-1980	10-1-1985
	35th Infantry Division	10-1-1985	10-1-2000
	Barbourville Kentucky	10-1-1980	
	35th Infantry Division		

151st Infantry Regiment-National Guard

1-151	38th Infantry Division	2-1-1959	2-1-1968
	New Albany Indiana	2-1-1968	3-1-1977
	38th Infantry Division	3-1-1977	9-1-1994
	76th Infantry Brigade	9-1-1994	
	38th Infantry Division		
2-151	38th Infantry Division	2-1-1959	2-1-1968
	38th Infantry Division	3-1-1977	10-1-1999
D-151	Evansville Indiana	12-1-1967	5-13-1968
	Fort Benning Georgia	5-13-1968	11-28-1969
	2nd Field Force Vietnam	11-28-1969	11-20-1969
	38th Infantry Division	11-20-1969	3-1-1977
E-151	Muncie Indiana	12-1-1967	3-17-1971
F-151	South Bend Indiana (LAT)	- -2004	
G-151	Elkhart Indiana (LAT)	- -2004	
H-151	Plmouth Indiana (LAT)	- -2004	

152nd Infantry Regiment-National Guard

1-152	38th Infantry Division	2-1-1959	9-1-1994
	76th Infantry Brigade	9-1-1994	
	38th Infantry Division		
2-152	38th Infantry Division	2-1-1959	

153rd Infantry Regiment-National Guard

1-153	39th Infantry Division	6-1-1959	12-1-1967
	39th Infantry Brigade	12-1-1967	
	36th Infantry Division		
2-153	39th Infantry Division	6-1-1959	12-1-1967
	39th Infantry Brigade	12-1-1967	
	36th Infantry Division		
3-153	39th Infantry Brigade	12-1-1967	

155th Infantry Regiment-National Guard

1-155	31st Infantry Division	5-1-1959	2-15-1968
	30th Armored Division	2-15-1968	11-1-1973
	155th Armored Brigade	11-1-1973	
	36th Infantry Division		
2-155	31st Infantry Division	5-1-1959	2-15-1968
3-155	31st Infantry Division	5-1-1959	2-15-1968

156th Infantry Regiment-National Guard

1-156	39th Infantry Division	7-1-1959	12-1-1967
	256th Infantry Brigade	12-1-1967	3-1-1977
2-156	39th Infantry Division	7-1-1959	12-1-1967
	256th Infantry Brigade	12-1-1967	
	36th Infantry Division		
3-156	39th Infantry Division	7-1-1959	12-1-1967
	256th Infantry Brigade	12-1-1967	
	36th Infantry Division		
4-156	39th Infantry Division	3-1-1963	12-1-1967
	Louisiana	9-1-1991	9-1-1993

158th Infantry Regiment-National Guard

1-158	258th Infantry Brigade	3-1-1959	12-1-1967
	40th Infantry Division		
2-158	258th Infantry Brigade	3-1-1959	12-1-1967
3-158	258th Infantry Brigade	3-1-1959	12-1-1967

159th Infantry Regiment-National Guard

1-159	49th Infantry Division	5-1-1959	12-4-1965
	49th Infantry Brigade	12-4-1965	1-13-1974
	40th Infantry Division	1-13-1974	1-1-1976
2-159	49th Infantry Division	5-1-1959	12-4-1965
	49th Infantry Brigade	12-4-1965	1-13-1974
	40th Infantry Division	1-13-1974	10-1-2000

160th Infantry Regiment-National Guard

1-160	40th Armored Division	7-1-1959	1-29-1968
	40th Infantry Brigade	1-29-1968	1-13-1974
	40th Infantry Division	1-13-1974	8-1-1985
	40th Infantry Division	10-1-2000	
2-160	40th Armored Division	7-1-1959	1-29-1968
	40th Infantry Brigade	1-29-1968	1-13-1974
	40th Infantry Division	1-13-1974	10-1-2000
3-160	40th Armored Division	7-1-1959	1-29-1968
	40th Infantry Brigade	1-29-1968	1-13-1974
	40th Infantry Division	1-13-1974	
4-160	40th Armored Division	7-1-1959	11-1-1965
	29th Infantry Brigade	11-1-1965	1-29-1968
	40th Armored Brigade	1-29-1968	1-13-1974
	40th Infantry Division	1-13-1974	10-1-2000

161st Infantry Regiment-National Guard

1-161	41st Infantry Division	4-15-1959	3-1-1968
	81st Infantry Brigade	3-1-1968	
	40th Infantry Division		
2-161	41st Infantry Division	4-15-1959	3-1-1968
	81st Infantry Brigade	3-1-1968	5-1-1971
	Washington	5-1-1971	5-1-1974
3-161	81st Infantry Brigade	3-1-1968	10-1-1994

162nd Infantry Regiment-National Guard

1-162	41st Infantry Division	4-1-1959	11-1-1965
	41st Infantry Brigade	11-1-1965	
2-162	41st Infantry Division	4-1-1959	11-1-1965
	41st Infantry Brigade	11-1-1965	
	40th Infantry Division		

163rd Infantry Regiment-National Guard

1-163	163rd Armored Brigade	2-1-1989	10-1-1995
	116th Cavalry Brigade	10-1-1995	
	34th Infantry Division		

165th Infantry Regiment-National Guard

1-165	42nd Infantry Division	3-16-1959	4-15-1963

166th Infantry Regiment-National Guard

1-166	37th Infantry Division	9-1-1959	2-15-1968
	38th Infantry Division	2-15-1968	3-1-1977
	73rd Infantry Brigade	3-1-1977	9-1-1992

167th Infantry Regiment-National Guard

1-167	31st Infantry Division	5-2-1959	1-15-1968
	30th Armored Division	1-15-1968	11-1-1973
	31st Armored Brigade	11-1-1973	10-1-2000
	35th Infantry Division	10-1-2000	Present
2-167	31st Infantry Division	5-2-1959	4-1-1963

168th Infantry Regiment-National Guard

1-168	34th Infantry Division	5-1-1959	4-1-1963
	Council Bluffs Iowa	4-1-1963	3-1-1968
	47th Infantry Division	3-1-1968	2-10-1991
	34th Infantry Division	2-10-1991	
2-168	Altantis Iowa	4-1-1963	3-1-1968

36

169th Infantry Regiment-National Guard

1-169	43rd Infantry Division	5-1-1959	5-1-1963
	Connecticut	5-1-1963	12-16-1967
	26th Infantry Division	12-16-1967	4-15-1992
2-169	43rd Infantry Division	5-1-1959	5-1-1963
	Connecticut	5-1-1963	12-16-1967

170th Infantry Regiment-National Guard

1-170	29th Infantry Division	6-1-1986	10-1-1995

172nd Infantry Regiment-National Guard

1-172	43rd Infantry Division	3-1-1959	4-1-1963
	86th Infantry Brigade	4-1-1963	2-1-1964
A-172	Jericho Vermont (MTN)	4-1-1983	10-1-1984
3-172	Jericho Vermont (MTN)	10-1-1984	
	42nd Infantry Division		

174th Infantry Regiment-National Guard

1-174	27th Armored Division	3-16-1959	2-1-1968
	50th Armored Division	2-1-1968	4-1-1975
	42nd Infantry Division	4-1-1975	9-1-1992
	42nd Infantry Division	4-1-1984	9-1-1991

175th Infantry Regiment-National Guard

1-175	29th Infantry Division	3-1-1959	2-1-1968
	28th Infantry Division	2-1-1968	4-1-1975
	58th Infantry Brigade	4-1-1975	7-1-1986
	29th Infantry Division	7-1-1986	Present
2-175	29th Infantry Division	3-1-1959	2-1-1968
	28th Infantry Division	2-1-1968	4-1-1975
	58th Infantry Brigade	4-1-1975	7-1-1986
	29th Infantry Division	7-1-1986	10-1-1995
H-175	Not Confirmed		

176th Infantry Regiment-National Guard

1-176	Richmond Virginia	6-1-1959	4-1-1963

178th Infantry Regiment-National Guard

1-178	Chicago Illinois	3-1-1959	2-1-1968
	33rd Infantry Brigade	2-1-1968	9-1-1995
	Chicago Illinois	9-1-1995	9-1-1997
	34th Infantry Division	9-1-1997	9-1-1998
	Chicago Illinois	9-1-1998	10-1-1999
	35th Infantry Division	10-1-1999	Present
2-178	Chicago Illinois	4-1-1963	2-1-1968

179th Infantry Regiment-National Guard

1 179	45th Infantry Division	5-1-1959	1-2-1968
	45th Infantry Brigade	1-2-1968	
	35th Infantry Division		
2-179	45th Infantry Division	5-1-1959	1-2-1968

180th Infantry Regiment-National Guard

1-180	45th Infantry Division	5-1-1959	1-2-1968
	45th Infantry Brigade	1-2-1968	
	35th Infantry Division		
2-180	45th Infantry Division	5-1-1959	1-2-1968
	Oklahoma	4-1-1977	9-1-1993

181st Infantry Regiment-National Guard

1-181	26th Infantry Division	5-1-1959	9-1-1993
	26th Infantry Brigade	9-1-1993	10-1-1995
	29th Infantry Division	10-1-1995	
	42nd Infantry Division		
2-181	26th Infantry Division	4-1-1975	9-1-1993

182nd Infantry Regiment-National Guard

1-182	26th Infantry Division	5-1-1959	9-1-1993
	42nd Infantry Division	9-1-1993	
2-182	26th Infantry Division	4-1-1975	2-1-1988

38

183rd Infantry Regiment-National Guard

| 1-183 | 29th Infantry Division | 6-1-1986 | 10-1-1995 |

184th Infantry Regiment-National Guard

1-184	49th Infantry Division	5-1-1959	12-4-1965
	49th Infantry Brigade	12-4-1965	11-1-1976
	40th Infantry Division	11-1-1976	9-1-1995
	29th Infantry Brigade	9-1-1995	
	40th Infantry Division		
2-184	49th Infantry Division	5-1-1959	1-29-1968

185th Infantry Regiment-National Guard

1-185	49th Infantry Division	5-1-1959	1-29-1968
	40th Infantry Division	10-1-2000	Present
2-185	49th Infantry Division	3-1-1963	1-29-1968
	California	1-29-1968	1-13-1974

186th Infantry Regiment-National Guard

1-186	41st Infantry Division	4-1-1959	11-1-1965
	41st Infantry Brigade	11-1-1965	
	40th Infantry Division		
2-186	41st Infantry Division	4-1-1959	3-1-1968

187th Infantry Regiment-Active Component

1-187	11th Airborne Division	3-1-1957	7-1-1958
	24th Infantry Division	7-1-1958	2-8-1959
	82nd Airborne Division	2-8-1959	3-6-1964
	Fort Bragg North Carolina	3-6-1964	5-24-1964
	11th Air Assault Division	2-1-1964	6-30-1965
	193rd Infantry Brigade	10-1-1983	5-1-1987
	101st Airborne Division	9-16-1987	Present
2-187	101st Airborne Division	4-25-1957	2-1-1964
	193rd Infantry Brigade	10-1-1983	5-1-1987
3-187	11th Air Assault Division	2-7-1963	2-1-1964
	101st Airborne Division	2-1-1964	Present
4-187	101st Airborne Division	10-1-183	9-16-1987
5-187	101st Airborne Division	10-1-1983	9-16-1987

188th Infantry Regiment-Active Component

| 1-188 | 11th Air Assault Division | 7-18-1963 | 6-30-1965 |
| E-188 | Fort Benning Georgia | 7-15-1965 | 11-6-1965 |

194th Infantry Regiment-National Guard

| 1-194 | 34th Infantry Division | 9-1-1993 | 10-1-2000 |

200th Infantry Regiment-National Guard

1-200	31st Infantry Division	5-2-1959	1-15-1968
	42nd Infantry Division		
2-200	31st Infantry Division	5-2-1959	1-15-1968
	29th Infantry Division		
E-200	Mobile Alabama	12-1-1969	2-1-1972

211th Infantry Regiment-National Guard

| 1-211 | 51st Infantry Division | 4-15-1959 | 4-16-1963 |
| 2-211 | 51st Infantry Division | 4-15-1959 | 4-16-1963 |

220th Infantry Regiment-National Guard

| 1-220 | 26th Infantry Division | 5-1-1959 | 4-1-1975 |

225th Infantry Regiment-National Guard

1-225	46th Infantry Division	3-16-1959	2-1-1968
	Detroit Michigan	2-1-1968	3-1-1977
	38th Infantry Division	3-1-1977	9-1-1993

242nd Infantry Regiment-National Guard

| 1-242 | 42nd Infantry Division | 4-1-1975 | 4-1-1984 |

249th Infantry Regiment-National Guard

| 1-249 | Oregon | 4-1-1980 | 9-1-1993 |

251st Infantry Regiment-National Guard
| 1-251 | 42nd Infantry Division | 3-16-1959 | 4-15-1963 |

259th Infantry Regiment-National Guard

A-259	Wilmington Delaware	1-1-1971	6-1-1974

279th Infantry Regiment-National Guard

1-279	45th Infantry Division	5-1-1959	1-2-1968
	45th Infantry Brigade	1-2-1968	
2-279	45th Infantry Division	5-1-1959	1-2-1968

293rd Infantry Regiment-National Guard

1-293	38th Infantry Division	2-1-1959	9-1-1994
	76th Infantry Brigade	9-1-1994	
	38th Infantry Division		
2-293	38th Infantry Division	2-1-1959	10-1-1999
E-293	Logansport Indiana (LAT)	- -2004	
F-293	Peru Indiana (LAT)	- -2004	
G-293	Frankfort Indiana (LAT)	- -2004	

294th Infantry Regiment-National Guard

1-294	Barrigada Guam	10-1-1987	
	40th Infantry Division		

295th Infantry Regiment-National Guard

1-295	92nd Infantry Brigade	2-15-1959	
2-295	92nd Infantry Brigade	5-1-1964	2-1-1968

296th Infantry Regiment-National Guard

1-296	92nd Infantry Brigade	2-1-1959	
	29th Infantry Division		
2-296	92nd Infantry Brigade	5-1-1964	2-1-1968

297th Infantry Regiment-National Guard

1-297	Alaska	2-1-1959	10-1-1976
	207th Infantry Group	10-1-1976	
	40th Infantry Division		
2-297	Alaska	2-1-1959	10-1-1976
	207th Infantry Group	10-1-1976	

3-297	Alaska	2-1-1959	5-1-1972
	207th Infantry Group	10-1-1976	
4-297	207th Infantry Group	11-1-1978	9-1-1993
5-297	207th Infantry Group	10-1-1976	9-30-1974
6-297	207th Infantry Group	9-1-1993	9-30-1974

207th Infantry Group is (Arctic Reconnaissance)

299th Infantry Regiment-National Guard

1-299	29th Infantry Brigade	2-15-1959	10-1-1995
2-299	29th Infantry Brigade	2-15-1959	
3-299	29th Infantry Brigade	4-1-1963	11-15-1965

305th Infantry Regiment-Army Reserve

1-305	77th Infantry Division	5-1-1959	12-30-1965
2-305	77th Infantry Division	3-26-1963	12-30-1965

306th Infantry Regiment-Army Reserve

1-306	77th Infantry Division	5-1-1959	12-30-1965
2-306	77th Infantry Division	3-26-1963	12-30-1965

307th Infantry Regiment-Army Reserve

1-307	77th Infantry Division	5-1-1959	12-30-1965
	77th Infantry Division	3-26-1963	12-30-1965

313th Infantry Regiment-Army Reserve

1-313	79th Infantry Division	4-6-1959	1-7-1963
	157th Infantry Brigade	1-7-1963	2-1-1975

314th Infantry Regiment-Army Reserve

1-314	79th Infantry Division	4-6-1959	1-7-1963
	157th Infantry Brigade	1-7-1963	9-1-1995

315th Infantry Regiment-Army Reserve

1-315	79th Infantry Division	4-6-1959	1-7-1963
	157th Infantry Brigade	1-7-1963	10-1-1973
	Pennsylvania	10-1-1973	3-1-1974
	157th Infantry Brigade	3-1-1974	9-1-1995

322nd Infantry Regiment-Army Reserve

| 1-322 | 81st Infantry Division | 5-1-1959 | 12-31-1965 |
| 2-322 | 81st Infantry Division | 4-1-1963 | 12-31-1965 |

325th Infantry Regiment-Active Component

1-325	82nd Airborne Division	9-1-1957	Present
2-325	82nd Airborne Division	5-24-1964	Present
3-325	82nd Airborne Division	5-24-1964	5-1-1986
	Southern European Task Force	5-1-1986	2-15-1996
	82nd Airborne Division	2-15-1996	5-26-2006
4-325	82nd Airborne Division	7-15-1968	12-15-1969
	82nd Airborne Division	5-1-1986	2-15-1996
E-325	82nd Airborne Division	12-21-1977	

327th Infantry Regiment-Active Component

1-327	101st Airborne Division	4-25-1957	Present
2-327	101st Airborne Division	2-3-1964	Present
3-327	101st Airborne Division	1-21-1983	10-16-2005
4-327	172nd Infantry Brigade	1-21-1983	4-15-1986
5-327	172nd Infantry Brigade	1-21-1983	4-15-1986
6-327	172nd Infantry Brigade	1-21-1983	4-15-1986

345th Infantry Regiment-Army Reserve

| 1-345 | 81st Infantry Division | 5-1-1959 | 12-31-1965 |
| 2-345 | 81st Infantry Division | 4-1-1963 | 12-31-1965 |

357th Infantry Regiment-Army Reserve

| 1-357 | 90th Infantry Division | 4-1-1959 | 12-31-1965 |
| 2-357 | 90th Infantry Division | 3-15-1963 | 12-31-1965 |

358th Infantry Regiment-Army Reserve

1-358	90th Infantry Division	4-1-1959	12-31-1965
2-358	90th Infantry Division	3-15-1963	12-31-1965

359th Infantry Regiment-Army Reserve

1-359	90th Infantry Division	4-1-1959	12-31-1965
2-359	90th Infantry Division	3-15-1963	12-31-1965

380th Infantry Regiment-National Guard

1-380	Washington D.C.	2-1-1972	10-1-1975

381st Infantry Regiment-Army Reserve

1-381	96th Infantry Division	6-1-1959	3-15-1963

383rd Infantry Regiment-Army Reserve

1-383	96th Infantry Division	6-1-1959	3-15-1963

409th Infantry Regiment-Army Reserve

1-409	103rd Infantry Division	5-18-1959	3-15-1963
	205th Infantry Brigade	3-15-1963	8-15-1994

410th Infantry Regiment-Army Reserve

1-410	103rd Infantry Division	5-18-1959	3-15-1963
	205th Infantry Brigade	3-15-1963	8-15-1994

411th Infantry Regiment-Army Reserve

1-411	103rd Infantry Division	5-18-1959	3-15-1963

425th Infantry Regiment-National Guard

E-425	Pontiac Michigan	2-1-1968	2-1-1972
F-425	Detroit Michigan	2-1-1968	2-1-1972
	Pontiac Michigan	2-1-1972	Present

442nd Infantry Regiment-Army Reserve

100-442	Fort De Russy Hawaii	5-29-1959	12-17-1967
	29th Infantry Brigade	12-17-1967	
	40th Infantry Division		
E-442	Hawaii		

501st Infantry Regiment-Active Component

1-501	101st Airborne Division	4-25-1957	1-21-1983
	6th Infantry Division	12-1-1983	4-17-1998
	172nd Infantry Brigade	4-17-1998	3-16-2004
	Alaska	3-16-2004	7-16-2005
	25th Infantry Division	7-16-2005	Present
2-502	82nd Airborne Division	9-1-1957	2-3-1964
	101st Airborne Division	2-3-1964	1-14-1972

502nd Infantry Regiment-Active Component

1-502	101st Airborne Division	4-25-1957	Present
2-502	11th Airborne Division	3-1-1957	7-1-1958
	101st Airborne Division	2-3-1964	1-21-1983
	101st Airborne Division	6-5-1984	Present
3-502	101st Airborne Division	6-5-1984	9-15-2004
4-502	Berlin Brigade	9-16-1987	10-15-1992
5-502	Berlin Brigade	9-16-1987	10-15-1994
6-502	Berlin Brigade	9-16-1987	10-15-1994

503rd Infantry Regiment-Active Component

1-503	11th Airborne Division	3-1-1957	7-1-1958
	24th Infantry Division	7-1-1958	1-7-1959
	82nd Airborne Division	1-7-1959	3-26-1963
	173rd Airborne Brigade	3-26-1963	1-14-1972
	101st Airborne Division	1-14-1972	11-6-1984
	2nd Infantry Division	12-16-1986	11-15-2005
	173rd Airborne Brigade	6-15-2006	Present
2-503	82nd Airborne Division	9-1-1957	6-24-1960
	25th Infantry Division	6-24-1960	7-1-1961
	173rd Airborne Brigade	3-26-1963	1-14-1972

	101st Airborne Division	1-14-1972	10-1-1983
	2nd Infantry Division	12-16-1986	9-29-1990
	173rd Airborne Brigade	12-16-2001	Present
3-503	173rd Airborne Brigade	4-1-1967	1-14-1972
4-503	173rd Airborne Brigade	4-1-1966	1-14-1972

504th Infantry Regiment-Active Component

1-504	82nd Airborne Division	9-1-1957	12-11-1958
	8th Infantry Division	12-11-1958	4-1-1963
	82nd Airborne Division	4-1-1963	Present
2-504	11th Airborne Division	3-1-1957	7-1-1958
	82nd Airborne Division	7-1-1960	Present
3-504	82nd Airborne Division	7-15-1968	12-15-1969
	82nd Airborne Division	5-1-1986	
E-504	82nd Airborne Division	12-21-1977	

505th Infantry Regiment-Active Component

1-505	82nd Airborne Division	9-1-1957	1-15-1959
	8th Infantry Division	1-15-1959	4-1-1963
	82nd Airborne Division	4-1-1963	Present
2-505	11th Airborne Division	3-1-1957	7-1-1958
	82nd Airborne Division	5-24-1964	Present
3-505	82nd Airborne Division	7-15-1968	12-15-1969
	82nd Airborne Division	10-3-1986	
E-505	82nd Airborne Division	12-21-1977	

506th Infantry Regiment-Active Component

1-506	101st Airborne Division	4-25-1957	1-21-1983
	2nd Infantry Division	8-16-1987	10-16-2005
	101st Airborne Division	10-16-2005	Present
2-506	101st Airborne Division	2-3-1964	1-14-1972
	101st Airborne Division	10-16-2005	Present
3-506	101st Airborne Division	4-1-1967	1-14-1972

507th Infantry Regiment-Active Component

1-507	Fort Benning Georgia	T	10-23-1985	Present

508th Infantry Regiment-Active Component

1-508	82nd Airborne Division	5-24-1964	5-25-1986
	193rd Infantry Brigade	7-10-1986	10-15-1994
	Southern European Task Force	4-27-1996	6-12-2000
	173rd Airborne Brigade	6-12-2000	5-26-2006
	82nd Airborne Division	5-26-2006	Present
2-508	82nd Airborne Division	5-24-1964	4-30-1986
	82nd Airborne Division	6-16-2006	Present
3-508	193rd Infantry Brigade	8-8-1962	6-28-1968

509th Infantry Regiment-Active Component

1-509	8th Infantry Division	4-1-1963	8-31-1973
	Southern European Task Force	8-31-1973	5-1-1986
	Little Rock AFB Arkansas	12-18-1987	5-31-1993
	Fort Polk Louisiana	1-15-1994	Present
2-509	8th Infantry Division	4-1-1963	8-31-1973
C-509	Fort Rucker Alabama	7-1-1975	5-31-1993
3-509	Germany	1-15-1973	8-31-1973
	25th Infantry Division	9-16-2005	Present

511th Infantry Regiment-Active Component

1-511	11th Air Assault Division	7-18-1963	6-30-1965
HHC	Fort Benning Georgia	11-2-1965	11-16-1965
A-511	Fort Bragg North Carolina	10-11-1997	Present

II. Artillery Battalions 1957-2011 (AD & Field)

1st Air Defense Artillery Regiment-Active Component

1-1	Germany	9-13-1972	
	108th ADA Brigade	6-16-1987	7-15-1991
2-1	Germany	9-13-1972	6-30-1983
	11th ADA Brigade	6-16-1987	9-15-1994
	35th ADA Brigade	5-4-1996	Present
3-1	Irwin Pennsylvania	9-1-1958	9-30-1974
	94th ADA Brigade	6-16-1987	9-15-1993
4-1	Edgewood Maryland	9-1-1958	9-1-1971
	94th ADA Brigade	6-16-1987	7-15-1993
5-1	Germany	9-1-1971	9-13-1972
6-1	Non-Active	9-1-1971	
7-1	Non-Active	9-1-1971	
8-1	Fort Bliss Texas	9-24-1960	--------------
	Oakland Army Base California	--------------	6-12-1973
9-1	Non-Active	9-1-1971	
16D-1	Germany	9-1-1958	7-20-1960

1st Field Artillery Regiment-Active Component

1-1	United States Military Academy	5-15-1958	Present
2-1	4th Infantry Division	4-1-1957	10-1-1963
	Fort Sill Oklahoma	8-25-1966	7-31-1972
	1st Armored Division	1-16-1988	1-17-1992
3-1	Oakdale Pennsylvania	9-1-1958	9-1-1971
	1st Armored Division	1-16-1988	1-17-1992
	3rd Infantry Division	1-17-1992	2-16-1996
4-1	Edgewood Maryland	9-1-1958	9-1-1971
	5th Infantry Division	1-16-1988	12-15-1992
	1st Armored Division	2-15-1996	Present
5-1	Germany	9-1-1958	9-1-1971
	5th Infantry Division	1-16-1988	12-15-1992
6-1	79th Infantry Division	3-22-1959	2-15-1963
	6th Infantry Division	11-24-1967	7-24-1968
	Fort Campbell Kentucky	7-24-1967	7-21-1969

48

	1st Armored Division	1-16-1988	1-17-1992
	3rd Infantry Division	1-17-1992	1-15-1994
7-1	83rd Infantry Division	3-20-1959	12-31-1965
	Chicago Illinois	9-1-1971	9-1-1974
	Addison Illinois	9-1-1974	12-18-1979
	Chicago Illinois	12-18-1979	9-1-1996
8-1	Fort Bliss Texas	9-24-1960	9-1-1971
9-1	25th Infantry Division	7-1-1960	7-17-1963
	Schofield Barracks Hawaii	7-17-1963	8-5-1963
	Fort Carson Colorado	8-25-1967	8-26-1968
	5th Infantry Division	- -1991	12-15-1992
	2nd Armored Division	12-15-1992	1-16-1996
	4th Infantry Division	1-16-1996	6-15-1998

2nd Air Defense Artillery Regiment-Active Component

1-2	South Korea	9-13-1972	7-15-1981
	108th ADA Brigade	3-16-1989	9-15-1997
2-2	Germany	9-13-1972	7-15-1981
	31st ADA Brigade	1-16-1989	7-15-1996
3-2	Fort Riley Kansas	3-17-1958	5-5-1959
	1st Corps	11-2-1988	7-15-1994
	31st ADA Brigade	10-16-1996	Present
4-2	Non-Active	9-1-1971	
5-2	Germany	9-1-1958	3-21-1960
	Fort Bliss Texas	6-1-1966	---------------
	South Vietnam	------------	6-23-1971
	69th ADA Brigade	8-16-1991	9-15-1997
6-2	Walker AFB New Mexico	4-25-1960	6-25-1960
7-2	Fort Bliss Texas	11-27-1960	---------------
	South Korea	---------------	9-13-1972
16D-2	South Korea	8-22-1958	1-22-1959

2nd Field Artillery Regiment-Active Component

1-2	8th Infantry Division	7-1-1957	8-1-1984
2-2	Fort Sill Oklahoma	6-25-1960	4-1-1980
	Fort Sill Oklahoma	8-1-1981	12-7-2006
	428th Field Artillery Brigade	12-7-2006	Present
3-2	Fort Riley Kansas	3-17-1958	5-5-1959

	1st Armored Division	2-3-1962	3-25-1969
4-2	96th Infantry Division	6-1-1959	2-15-1963
5-2	Germany	9-1-1958	8-10-1963
	Fort Bliss Texas	6-1-1966	11-1966
	23rd Artillery Group	11-1966	6-23-1971
6-2	Fort Hood Texas	11-24-1960	9-1-1971
7-2	South Korea	11-24-1960	9-1-1971

3rd Air Defense Artillery Regiment-Active Component

1-3	Fort Bliss Texas	7-10-1972	12-4-1972
	101st Airborne Division	12-4-1972	3-16-1988
	4th Infantry Division	7-16-1989	3-16-1996
	3rd Infantry Division	3-16-1996	6-21-2004
2-3	Selfridge AFB Michigan	9-13-1972	9-30-1974
	1st Infantry Division	7-16-1989	6-15-1996
3-3	5th Infantry Division	7-16-1989	11-24-1992
	2nd Armored Division	12-2-1992	2-16-1996
4-3	Detroit Michigan	9-1-1958	12-23-1960
	Fort Bliss Texas	7-1-1983	3-16-1989
	3rd Infantry Division	7-16-1989	2-15-1996
	1st Infantry Division	2-16-1996	9-15-2000
5-3	Oakdale Pennsylvania	9-1-1958	10-18-1963
	8th Infantry Division	7-16-1989	1-15-1992
	1st Armored Division	1-15-1992	2-18-1997
6-3	Chicago Illinois	9-1-1958	6-1-1966
	1st Armored Division	7-16-1989	1-15-1992
7-3	Non-Active	9-1-1971	
8-3	Oakland Army Base California	9-1-1971	6-12-1973
16D-3	Okinawa	9-1-1958	10-25-1961

3rd Field Artillery Regiment-Active Component

1-3	2nd Armored Division	7-1-1957	5-21-1991
	1st Cavalry Division	5-21-1991	11-29-1992
	2nd Armored Division	12-2-1992	3-16-1996
	1st Armored Division		Present
2-3	3rd Armored Division	10-1-1957	7-20-1991
	8th Infantry Division	7-20-1991	8-16-1991
	1st Armored Division	8-16-1991	Present

3-3	Fort Knox Kentucky	6-25-1958	4-15-1968
	194th Armored Brigade	12-21-1975	10-1-1983
	2nd Armored Division	10-1-1983	- -1990
4-3	Detroit Michigan	9-1-1958	12-23-1960
	1st Armored Division	2-3-1962	5-10-1971
	2nd Armored Division	10-1-1983	9-15-1992
5-3	Oakdale Pennsylvania	9-1-1958	10-18-1963
	6th Infantry Division	11-24-1967	7-24-1968
	42nd Field Artillery Brigade	10-1-1983	--------------
	72nd Field Artillery Brigade	--------------	--------------
	17th Field Artillery Brigade	--------------	Present
6-3	Chicago Illinois	9-1-1958	6-1-1965
7-3	Evanston Illinois	10-1-1959	1-31-1968
8-3	Fort Bliss Texas	9-1-1958	2-1-1961
	Okinawa	2-1-1961	-------------
	Oakland Army Base California	--------------	9-1-1971

4th Air Defense Artillery Regiment-Active Component

1-4	Niagara Falls New York	9-1-1958	3-31-1970
	Fort Lawton Washington	9-13-1972	4-30-1974
	Fort Lewis Washington	4-1-1979	4-16-1988
	1st Armored Division	2-18-1997	9-16-2004
2-4	Non-Active	9-1-1971	
3-4	82nd Airborne Division	9-13-1972	
4-4	Poulsbo Washington	9-1-1958	--------------
	Fort Lewis Washington	-------------	9-13-1972
5-4	Non-Active	9-1-1971	
6-4	Non-Active	9-1-1971	
7-4	Non-Active	9-1-1971	
8-4	Non-Active	9-1-1971	
16D-4	Fort Bliss Texas	9-1-1958	9-17-1962

4th Field Artillery Regiment-Active Component

1-4	Niagara Falls New York	9-1-1958	3-30-1970
	2nd Infantry Division	4-16-1987	4-15-1992
2-4	9th Infantry Division	12-1-1957	1-31-1962
	9th Infantry Division	2-1-1966	10-13-1970
	9th Infantry Division	10-21-1972	10-2-1986

	214th Field Artillery Brigade	6-16-1986	9-18-2006
	214th Fires Brigade	9-18-2006	Present
3-4	Fort Sill Oklahoma	6-25-1958	9-25-1958
	2nd Infantry Brigade	4-1-1960	4-20-1962
4-4	Fort Lawton Washington	12-26-1960	9-1-1971
	Fort Sill Oklahoma	9-13-1972	7-16-1988
5-4	5th Infantry Division	2-19-1962	8-27-1971
6-4	63rd Infantry Division	6-1-1959	12-31-1965
7-4	77th Infantry Division	5-1-1959	12-31-1965
8-4	1st Infantry Division	4-20-1960	10-23-1963
	Fort Sill Oklahoma	10-23-1963	1-2-1964
	Fort Sill Oklahoma	3-1-1967	8-13-1967
	108th Artillery Group	8-13-1967	9-1-1971
	Fort Sill Oklahoma	9-1-1971	9-13-1972

5th Air Defense Artillery Regiment-Active Component

1-5	Coventry Rhode Island	9-13-1972	10-30-1974
	24th Infantry Division	11-16-1988	4-25-1996
2-5	2nd Armored Division	9-13-1972	7-15-1991
3-5	Bedford Massachusetts	9-1-1958	--------------
	Coventry Rhode Island	------------	9-13-1972
	3rd Armored Division	6-16-1987	1-17-1992
4-5	Laytonville Maryland	9-1-1958	8-10-1960
	1st Cavalry Division	11-16-1988	7-15-2005
	31st ADA Brigade	7-15-2005	Present
5-5	2nd Infantry Division	11-16-1988	10-18-2005
	555th Brigade (ME)	10-18-2005	Present
6-5	Non-Active	9-1-1971	
F-5	South Korea	9-16-1988	
7-5	Non-Active	9-1-1971	
G-5	South Korea	9-16-1988	
16D-5	Fort Miles Delaware	9-1-1958	--------------
	Fort Meade Maryland	------------	12-24-1965

5th Field Artillery Regiment-Active Component

1-5	1st Infantry Division	2-15-1957	Present
2-5	Germany	6-25-1958	3-1-1983
	1st Infantry Division	3-1-1983	7-15-1991

	212th Field Artillery Brigade	4-15-1996	9-18-2006
	214th Fires Brigade	9-18-2006	Present
3-5	Coventry Rhode Island	9-1-1958	9-1-1971
	210th Field Artillery Brigade	3-1-1983	9-1-1991
	72nd Field Artillery Brigade	9-1-1991	9-1-1992
4-5	Laytonville Maryland	9-1-1958	12-26-1960
	1st Infantry Division	3-1-1983	2-15-1996
5-5	94th Infantry Division	5-1-1959	1-7-1963
	187th Infantry Brigade	1-7-1963	4-15-1994
6-5	77th Infantry Division	5-1-1959	12-31-1965
7-5	South Korea	9-1-1958	9-1-1971

6th Air Defense Artillery Regiment-Active Component

1-6	Fort Bliss Texas (T)	6-16-1987	Present
2-6	Fort Bliss Texas (T)	6-16-1987	Present
3-6	Fort Bliss Texas (T)	6-16-1987	Present
4-6	Germany	9-1-1958	3-26-1970
	Fort Bliss Texas T	6-16-1987	
5-6	Germany	9-1-1958	6-30-1982
6-6	Finleyville Pennsylvania	9-1-1958	7-26-1960
7-6	Non-Active	9-1-1971	
8-6	Non-Active	9-1-1971	

6th Field Artillery Regiment-Active Component

1-6	1st Infantry Division	2-15-1957	5-5-1971
	1st Cavalry Division	5-5-1971	6-21-1975
	Fort Bragg North Carolina	6-21-1975	10-1-1983
	1st Infantry Division	2-16-1996	- -2006
	1st Infantry Division	4-17-2007	Present
2-6	3rd Armored Division	10-1-1957	6-16-1988
B-6	1st Infantry Division	3-16-1987	9-15-1995
3-6	Fort Sill Oklahoma	6-25-1958	6-16-1966
	52nd Artillery Group	6-16-1966	4-10-1971
	1st Infantry Division	9-13-1972	3-16-1987
	10th Infantry Division	12-16-1995	Present
4-6	Germany	9-1-1958	3-26-1970
5-6	Germany	9-1-1958	9-1-1971
6-6	Finleyville Pennsylvania	9-1-1958	12-23-1960
7-6	79th Infantry Division	4-6-1959	2-28-1963
8-6	1st Infantry Division	2-15-1957	9-13-1972

7th Air Defense Artillery Regiment-Active Component

1-7	Fort Bliss Texas	9-13-1972	6-16-1987
	94th ADA Brigade	..12-16-1988	5-1-1998
	69th ADA Brigade	5-1-1998	7-1-1999
	108th ADA Brigade	7-1-1999	Present
2-7	11th ADA Brigade	12-16-1988	9-12-1996
3-7	Germany	9-1-1958	
4-7	Savannah Georgia	9-1-1958	1-23-1960
	Bergstrom AFB Texas	4-19-1960	6-25-1966
	35th ADA Brigade	12-16-1988	9-12-1996
5-7	Tappan New York	9-1-1958	11-30-1968
	94th ADA Brigade	12-16-1988	5-1-1998
	69th ADA Brigade	5-1-1998	
6-7	Non-Active	9-1-1971	
7-7	Non-Active	9-1-1971	
8-7	Fort Bliss Texas	9-1-1971	9-13-1972

7th Field Artillery Regiment-Active Component

1-7	1st Infantry Division	2-15-1957	4-16-1983
	10th Infantry Division	7-1-1986	12-15-1995
	1st Infantry Division	2-16-1996	Present
2-7	10th Infantry Division	7-1-1957	6-14-1958
	24th Infantry Division	4-1-1960	4-15-1970
	10th Infantry Division	7-1-1987	12-15-1995
3-7	Germany	9-1-1958	9-1-1971
	25th Infantry Division	7-16-1987	Present
4-7	Savannah Georgia	9-1-1958	1-23-1960
	Bergstrom AFB Texas	4-19-1960	6-25-1966
	42nd Field Artillery Brigade	4-16-1988	9-1-1991
5-7	Tappan New York	9-1-1958	11-30-1968
E-7	10th Infantry Division	9-1-1988	9-15-2004
6-7	77th Infantry Division	5-1-1959	12-31-1965
F-7	25th Infantry Division	11-13-1987	6-15-2005
7-7	94th Infantry Division	4-1-1959	12-31-1965
8-7	Fort Bliss Texas	4-9-1962	9-1-1991

54

8th Field Artillery Regiment-Active Component

1-8	25th Infantry Division	2-1-1957	9-15-1997
2-8	7th Infantry Division	7-1-1957	4-2-1971
	7th Infantry Division	4-21-1975	8-16-1995
	25th Infantry Division	8-16-1995	6-1-2006
	25th Infantry Division	12-16-2006	Present
3-8	81st Infantry Division	5-1-1959	12-31-1965
	18th Field Artillery Brigade	10-1-1983	1-16-1996
4-8	Pittsburgh Pennsylvania	4-1-1959	7-23-1976
	157th Infantry Brigade	7-23-1976	- -1991
5-8	103rd Infantry Division	5-18-1959	1-9-1963
	18th Field Artillery Brigade	10-1-1983	1-16-1996
6-8	Fort Sill Oklahoma	6-30-1959	2-1-1961
	South Korea	2-1-1961	10-26-1963
	Fort Carson Colorado	3-1-1967	12-31-1970
	7th Infantry Division	10-1-1983	8-15-1993
7-8	Fort Chaffee Arkansas	8-23-1963	6-29-1967
	23rd-54th Artillery Groups	6-29-1967	7-28-1971
	25th Infantry Division	10-1-1983	8-16-1995
8-8	2nd Infantry Division	10-1-1983	3-15-1996

9th Field Artillery Regiment-Active Component

1-9	3rd Infantry Division	7-1-1957	7-10-1962
	56th Field Artillery Command	1-17-1986	6-30-1991
	3rd Infantry Division	2-16-1996	Present
2-9	10th Infantry Division	7-1-1957	6-14-1958
	25th Infantry Division	4-1-1960	8-1-1967
	4th Infantry Division	8-1-1967	4-10-1970
	25th Infantry Division	12-11-1970	7-25-1972
	56th Field Artillery Command	1-17-1986	6-30-1991
3-9	83rd Infantry Division	3-20-1959	12-31-1965
	Fort Sill Oklahoma	9-1-1971	1-17-1986
	214th Field Artillery Brigade	1-17-1986	4-15-1996
4-9	79th Infantry Division	4-6-1959	2-28-1963
	56th Field Artillery Command	1-17-1986	6-30-1991
5-9	96th Infantry Division	6-1-1959	2-15-1963
6-9	Fort Sill Oklahoma	1-25-1963	---------------
	Germany	--------------	10-1-1983

7-9	Fort Irwin California	6-1-1966	10-23-1966
	23rd-54th Artillery Groups	10-23-1966	4-1-1970
	Fort Tilden New York	9-1-1971	9-23-1976
	Fort Lauderdale Florida	9-23-1976	3-1-1977
	Pampano Florida	3-1-1977	9-1-1995

10th Field Artillery Regiment-Active Component

1-10	3rd Infantry Division	7-1-1957	8-16-1986
	3rd Infantry Division	2-15-1996	Present
2-10	Fort Benning Georgia	5-25-1957	7-25-1958
	1st Infantry Brigade	7-25-1958	9-20-1962
	197th Infantry Brigade	9-20-1962	9-21-1975
	197th Infantry Brigade	6-21-1976	8-16-1986
3-10	Glasgow Montana	5-1-1959	12-20-1965
C-10	4th Infantry Division	3-16-1987	3-15-1996
4-10	81st Infantry Division	5-1-1959	12-31-1965
5-10	94th Infantry Division	5-1-1959	12-31-1965
6-10	Fort Sill Oklahoma	4-1-1963	----------------
	Germany	------------	5-16-1988

11th Field Artillery Regiment-Active Component

1-11	9th Infantry Division	12-1-1957	1-31-1962
	9th Infantry Division	2-1-1966	9-25-1969
	9th Infantry Division	10-21-1972	2-16-1991
	199th Infantry Brigade	2-16-1991	7-16-1992
2-11	Fort Campbell Kentucky	6-25-1958	12-31-1965
	23rd Artillery Group	12-31-1965	6-10-1968
	101st Airborne Division	6-10-1968	1-1-1972
	25th Infantry Division	9-13-1972	Present
3-11	24th Infantry Division	4-1-1960	4-15-1970
	9th Infantry Division	10-2-1986	2-16-1991
	210th Field Artillery Brigade	2-16-1991	9-1-1995
4-11	96th Infantry Division	6-1-1959	2-15-1963
	191st Infantry Brigade	2-15-1963	2-1-1964
	Salt Lake City Utah	2-1-1964	2-28-1968
	6th Infantry Division	10-2-1986	4-17-1998
	172nd Infantry Brigade	4-17-1998	11-16-2006
5-11	63rd Infantry Division	6-1-1959	12-31-1965
6-11	94th Infantry Division	5-1-1959	3-1-1963

	11th Infantry Brigade	7-1-1966	2-15-1969
	23rd Infantry Division	2-15-1969	11-30-1971
	9th Infantry Division	10-2-1986	8-15-1988
7-11	25th Infantry Division	4-1-1960	9-13-1972
G-11	6th Infantry Division	9-17-1989	4-15-1994

12th Field Artillery Regiment-Active Component

1-12	2nd Infantry Division	6-20-1957	2-20-1971
	Fort Sill Oklahoma	2-20-1971	7-16-1987
	75th Field Artillery Brigade	7-16-1987	--------------
	17th Field Artillery Brigade	-------------	9-16-2006
2-12	8th Infantry Division	5-1-1960	4-1-1963
	23rd Artillery Group	9-13-1969	8-29-1971
	Fort Sill Oklahoma	4-1-1976	9-15-1984
	210th Field Artillery Brigade	7-16-1987	--------------
	42nd Field Artillery Brigade	-------------	4-15-1992
	2nd Infantry Division	6-1-2006	Present
3-12	90th Infantry Division	5-1-1959	12-31-1965
	72nd Field Artillery Brigade	7-16-1987	- -1991
4-12	81st Infantry Division	5-1-1959	12-31-1965
	17th Field Artillery Brigade	7-16-1987	- -1991
5-12	77th Infantry Division	5-1-1959	12-30-1965
6-12	Fort Sill Oklahoma	4-15-1963	6-21-1971
8-12	Fort Bragg North Carolina	2-21-1968	8-28-1968

13th Field Artillery Regiment-Active Component

1-13	24th Infantry Division	6-5-1958	3-16-1970
	24th Infantry Division	11-21-1975	3-16-1987
A-13	24th Infantry Division	3-16-1987	2-15-1996
	3rd Infantry Division	2-15-1996	6-14-2000
2-13	Fort Sill Oklahoma	6-25-1958	10-30-1965
	23rd Artillery Group	10-30-1965	3-16-1970
	24th Infantry Division	9-21-1975	1-23-1976
3-13	25th Infantry Division	4-1-1960	10-1-1983
	214th Field Artillery Brigade	1-16-1996	9-18-2006
	75th Fires Brigade	9-18-2006	Present
4-13	102nd Infantry Division	6-1-1959	12-31-1965
5-13	Fort Wayne Indiana	7-15-1959	12-31-1968

	25th Infantry Division	12-6-1969	12-15-1970
6-13	103rd Infantry Division	5-18-1959	3-15-1963
7-13	Fort Irwin California	6-1-1966	10-28-1965
	41st Artillery Group	10-28-1965	10-13-1970

14th Field Artillery Regiment-Active Component

1-14	2nd Armored Division	7-1-1957	5-12-1967
	198th Infantry Brigade	5-12-1967	2-15-1969
	23rd Infantry Division	2-15-1969	11-30-1971
	2nd Armored Division	11-30-1971	10-1-1983
	Fort Stewart Georgia	3-1-1987	9-15-1990
	2nd Armored Division	12-16-1992	1-15-1996
	214th Field Artillery Brigade	1-15-1996	9-18-2006
	214th Fires Brigade	9-18-2006	Present
2-14	4th Armored Division	4-1-1957	5-10-1971
	1st Armored Division	5-10-1971	9-13-1972
	72nd Field Artillery Brigade	3-16-1988	1-15-1992
3-14	103rd Infantry Division	5-18-1959	3-15-1963
	205th Infantry Brigade	3-15-1963	4-15-1994
4-14	102nd Infantry Division	6-1-1959	4-1-1963
	Fort Sill Oklahoma	8-25-1966	5-31-1971
	72nd Field Artillery Brigade	5-16-1988	9-15-1991
5-14	83rd Infantry Division	3-20-1959	12-31-1965
	2nd Armored Division	6-19-1967	11-30-1971
6-14	Fort Sill Oklahoma	4-15-1963	10-29-1965
	52nd Artillery Group	10-29-1965	12-4-1970
	1st Armored Division	9-13-1972	1-16-1988

15th Field Artillery Regiment-Active Component

1-15	2nd Infantry Division	6-14-1958	Present
2-15	Fort Wainwright Alaska	6-20-1957	12-16-1967
	Fort Wainwright Alaska	6-1-1960	5-20-1963
	171st Infantry Brigade	5-20-1963	6-30-1972
B-15	Fort Wainwright Alaska	12-16-1857	6-1-1960
	7th Infantry Division	4-2-1986	9-15-1993
3-15	79th Infantry Division	4-6-1959	1-7-1963
	157th Infantry Brigade	1-7-1963	7-26-1976
	Fort McCellan Alabama	7-23-1976	9-1-1994

58

4-15	90th Infantry Division	4-1-1959	12-31-1965
5-15	83rd Infantry Division	3-20-1959	12-31-1965
	Fort Ord California	10-1-1984	9-15-1990
6-15	7th Infantry Division	7-1-1960	7-1-1963
	Fort Sill Oklahoma	11-1-1966	5-12-1967
	1st Infantry Division	5-12-1967	7-15-1968
	41st Artillery Group	7-15-1968	11-22-1969
7-15	Fort Bragg North Carolina	9-17-1962	7-1-1967
	41st-52nd Artillery Groups	7-1-1967	11-28-1971
	Fort Lewis Washington	11-28-1971	7-31-1972
8-15	Fort Bliss Texas	4-19-1961	--------------
	Homestead AFB Florida	-------------	9-1-1971

16th Field Artillery Regiment-Active Component

1-16	2nd Armored Division	7-1-1957	6-15-1972
	2nd Armored Division	3-1-1975	3-30-1979
2-16	4th Armored Division	4-1-1957	5-10-1971
	1st Armored Division	5-10-1971	6-21-1973
3-16	Fort Bragg North Carolina	6-21-1958	6-9-1967
	54th Artillery Group	6-9-1967	8-1968
	23rd Artillery Group	8-1968	11-2-1971
	8th Infantry Division	9-13-1972	8-15-1991
	4th Infantry Division	12-15-1995	Present
C-16	8th Infantry Division	8-16-1987	1-15-1992
4-16	81st Infantry Division	5-1-1959	4-1-1963
5-16	4th Infantry Division	5-6-1959	4-26-1971
6-16	Fort Chaffee Arkansas	8-23-1962	8-26-1968
F-16	108th Artillery Group	8-26-1968	4-1-1970
7-16	8th Infantry Division	5-1-1960	9-13-1972

17th Field Artillery Regiment-Active Component

1-17	Germany	6-1-1958	--------------
	South Korea	------------	--------------
	Fort Sill Oklahoma	------------	7-16-1987
	75th Field Artillery Brigade	7-16-1987	9-18-2006
	75th Fires Brigade	9-18-2006	Present
2-17	Fort Sill Oklahoma	6-25-1958	9-15-1965
	2nd Infantry Division	9-13-1972	Present
	41st Artillery Group	9-15-1965	4-26-1971

3-17	Nurnberg Germany	6-25-1958	3-1-1983
	210th Field Artillery Brigade	7-16-1987	1-15-1992
	214th Field Artillery Brigade	1-15-1992	9-16-1995
4-17	Raleigh North Carolina	5-1-1959	9-1-1995
5-17	90th Infantry Division	4-1-1959	12-31-1965
	214th Field Artillery Brigade	7-16-1987	3-15-1996
6-17	Bogalousa Alabama	4-1-1959	2-25-1963
7-17	2nd Infantry Division	5-2-1960	9-13-1972
8-17	Fort Campbell Kentucky	8-1-1967	--------------
	Fort Sill Oklahoma	------------	6-30-1971

18th Field Artillery Regiment-Active Component

1-18	Fort Sill Oklahoma	6-1-1958	6-25-1959
	Fort Sill Oklahoma	1-21-1961	7-16-1987
	17th Field Artillery Brigade	7-16-1987	- -1991
2-18	Fort Sill Oklahoma	6-1-1958	7-16-1987
	212th Field Artillery Brigade	7-16-1987	9-18-2006
	75th Fires Brigade	9-18-2006	Present
3-18	Fort Sill Oklahoma	6-25-1958	--------------
	Fort Lewis Washington	--------------	10-29-1965
	41st Artillery Group	10-29-1965	2-1-1968
	23rd Infantry Division	2-1-1968	10-1-1971
	Fort Sill Oklahoma	10-1-1971	7-16-1987
	212th Field Artillery Brigade	7-16-1987	8-25-2004
4-18	Fort Sill Oklahoma	6-1-1958	--------------
	Fort Lewis Washington	------------	10-8-1971
	41st Field Artillery Brigade	7-16-1987	1-15-1992
5-18	81st Infantry Division	5-1-1959	12-31-1965
	10th Infantry Division		
	75th Field Artillery Brigade	7-16-1987	4-15-1996
6-18	3rd Infantry Division	6-1-1960	4-18-1963
	Germany	4-18-1963	6-27-1963
	10th Infantry Division		
7-18	Fort Benning Georgia	12-23-1966	4-26-1968
	197th Infantry Brigade	4-26-1968	10-13-1970
G-18	Italy	6-25-1958	3-23-1959
H-18	Fort Knox Kentucky	12-12-1958	--------------
	Fort Rucker Alabama	----------------	3-24-1972

60

19th Field Artillery Regiment-Active Component

1-19	Fort Ord California	6-1-1957	4-25-1961
	5th Infantry Division	2-19-1962	12-15-1970
	4th Infantry Division	12-15-1970	4-1-1984
	USAFATC-Fort Sill Oklahoma (T)	2-28-1987	Present
2-19	1st Cavalry Division	10-15-1957	4-2-1971
	1st Cavalry Division	4-20-1974	3-20-1979
C-19	Keflavick Iceland	5-1-1958	-------------
	Fort Hamilton New York	------------	3-11-1960
3-19	1st Armored Division	2-3-1962	3-15-1971
	5th Infantry Division	6-21-1977	1-16-1988
4-19	90th Infantry Division	4-1-1959	12-31-1965
5-19	63rd Infantry Division	5-1-1959	12-31-1965

20th Field Artillery Regiment-Active Component

1-20	4th Infantry Division	5-6-1959	3-26-1969
	4th Infantry Division	3-1-1976	4-1-1984
	1st Cavalry Division	7-1-1988	- -1990
B-20	4th Infantry Division	1-16-1996	6-16-1998
2-20	1st Cavalry Division	10-15-1957	4-10-1971
	4th Infantry Division	9-13-1972	9-16-1980
	42nd Field Artillery Brigade	9-16-1987	6-15-1992
	4th Infantry Division	6-16-1998	9-16-2005
	4th Fires Brigade	9-16-2005	Present
3-20	103rd Infantry Division	5-18-1959	3-15-1963
	41st Field Artillery Brigade	3-16-1989	- -1991
4-20	Lansing Michigan	5-1-1959	9-1-1993
5-20	102nd Infantry Division	6-1-1959	12-31-1965
6-20	5th Infantry Division	2-19-1962	12-15-1970
	4th Infantry Division	12-15-1970	9-13-1972

21st Field Artillery Regiment-Active Component

1-21	1st Cavalry Division	7-1-1960	9-13-1972
	4th Infantry Division	9-13-1972	12-19-1973
	1st Cavalry Division	4-21-1975	7-2-1986
	1st Cavalry Division	9-16-1997	9-16-2005
	4th Fires Brigade	9-16-2005	Present

A-21	1st Cavalry Division	7-2-1986	9-15-1997
2-21	25th Infantry Division	2-1-1957	12-1-1968
	5th Infantry Division	7-21-1975	1-16-1988
3-21	Germany	7-1-1957	9-30-1974
	5th Infantry Division	6-21-1975	3-16-1987
C-21	5th Infantry Division	3-16-1987	11-24-1992
4-21	63rd Infantry Division	5-1-1959	12-31-1965
5-21	96th Infantry Division	6-1-1959	2-15-1963
6-21	5th Infantry Division	2-19-1962	12-15-1970
	4th Infantry Division	12-15-1970	9-13-1972

22nd Field Artillery Regiment-Active Component

1-22	4th Armored Division	4-1-1957	5-10-1971
	1st Armored Division	5-10-1971	1-16-1988
	USAFATC-Fort Sill Oklahoma	3-16-1996	Present
2-22	1st Armored Division	2-15-1957	12-23-1957
B-22	Fort Kobbe Canal Zone	4-1-1960	10-15-1962
	193rd Infantry Brigade	10-15-1962	10-2-1986
3-22	94th Infantry Division	5-1-1959	3-1-1963
	USAFATC-Fort Sill Oklahoma	2-28-1987	9-16-1990
4-22	81st Infantry Division	5-1-1959	12-31-1965
5-22	Little Rock Arkansas	4-1-1959	12-31-1965
	Fort Irwin California	5-15-1967	12-24-1967
	52nd Artillery Group	12-4-1967	12-4-1970

25th Field Artillery Regiment-Active Component

1-25	South Korea	6-25-1958	--------------
	Fort Bragg North Carolina	--------------	12-21-1976
A-25	Wertheim Germany	5-16-1987	4-15-1992
	41st Field Artillery Brigade	4-15-1992	9-15-1997
2-25	Germany	6-25-1958	9-20-1978
B-25	1st Armored Division	4-1-1984	5-16-1992
	3rd Infantry Division	5-16-1992	2-16-1996
	1st Infantry Division	2-16-1996	6-2-1999
3-25	Fort Sill Oklahoma	6-25-1958	12-23-1959
	Fort Chaffee Arkansas	8-23-1962	--------------
	Fort Sill Oklahoma	--------------	2-20-1971
C-25	214th Field Artillery Brigade	12-21-1976	- -1991

62

	1st Armored Division	2-15-1997	9-15-2000
D-25	Germany	6-24-1964	6-7-1967
	South Vietnam	9-25-1969	8-1-1970
	1st Infantry Division	12-21-1976	2-16-1996
4-25	10th Infantry Division	9-16-2004	Present
E-25	2nd Infantry Division	3-20-1978	6-16-1986
5-25	10th Infantry Division		Present
F-25	Fort Carson Colorado	1-25-1967	8-28-1968
8-25	Fort Bragg North Carolina (HHB)	6-27-1966	--------------
	South Vietnam	--------------	2-3-1971

26th Field Artillery Regiment-Active Component

1-26	Germany	12-2-1957	9-20-1978
A-26	4th Infantry Division	6-16-1986	6-19-1998
	4th Fires Brigade	9-16-2005	4-16-2007
	41st Fires Brigade	12-17-2004	Present
2-26	Fort Bragg North Carolina	6-21-1958	6-30-1971
B-26	82nd Airborne Division	12-21-1976	
	1st Cavalry Division	12-16-1992	9-15-1997
3-26	Fort Sill Oklahoma	6-25-1958	3-24-1972
C-26	2nd Armored Division	6-16-1986	5-21-1991
	75th Fires Brigade	9-18-2006	Present
4-26	Norman Oklahoma	4-1-1959	2-26-1963
D-26	25th Infantry Division	3-21-1978	8-15-1985
	18th Fires Brigade	6-17-2007	Present
E-26	11th Air Assault Division	6-24-1963	7-1-1965
F-26	Germany	9-25-1964	6-5-1967
	108th Artillery Group	2-5-1968	7-31-1971
	2nd Infantry Division	8-16-1986	4-15-2002
G-26	Fort Carson Colorado	1-25-1967	5-26-1967
8-26	Fort Sill Oklahoma (HHB)	7-15-1966	--------------
	Fort Lewis Washington	--------------	4-28-1971
H-26	214th Fires Brigade	9-16-2006	Present

27th Field Artillery Regiment-Active Component

1-27	1st Armored Division	2-15-1957	12-23-1957
	2nd Infantry Division	3-30-1960	2-20-1963
	Fort Sill Oklahoma	10-5-1966	4-1-1967

	23rd Artillery Group	4-1-1967	12-15-1970
	4th Infantry Division	12-15-1970	4-1-1984
	41st Field Artillery Brigade	3-16-1988	
2-27	3rd Armored Division	10-1-1957	6-16-1988
3-27	79th Infantry Division	4-6-1959	2-28-1963
	198th Infantry Brigade	5-10-1967	5-12-1967
	18th Field Artillery Brigade	3-1-1988	Present
4-27	83rd Infantry Division	3-20-1959	4-15-1963
	72nd Field Artillery Brigade	6-15-1985	--------------
	41st Field Artillery Brigade	--------------	--------------
	214th Field Artillery Brigade	--------------	1-15-1996
	1st Armored Division	2-15-1997	Present
5-27	Fort Lewis Washington	6-20-1963	11-3-1965
	41st Artillery Group	11-3-1965	8-31-1971
6-27	Fort Chaffee Arkansas	8-23-1962	11-3-1965
	23rd Artillery Group	11-3-1965	11-22-1971
	75th Field Artillery Brigade	10-1-1984	Present

28th Field Artillery Regiment-Active Component

1-28	8th Infantry Division	8-1-1957	7-10-1972
2-28	Fort Sill Oklahoma	6-1-1957	--------------
	Germany	-------------	
3-28	Germany	6-25-1958	4-1-1960
	9th Infantry Division	2-1-1966	7-28-1968
4-28	Fort Sill Oklahoma	7-22-1959	--------------
	Germany	--------------	10-25-1963
	Fort Sill Oklahoma	1-24-1966	9-19-1973
5-28	Cincinnati Ohio	6-1-1959	9-1-1993
6-28	Ponce Puerto Rico	7-7-1959	9-29-1959
	Mayaquez Puerto Rico	9-29-1959	3-31-1968
7-28	83rd Infantry Division	3-20-1959	12-31-1965

29th Field Artillery Regiment-Active Component

A-29	Fort Sill Oklahoma	6-25-1958	9-12-1960
1-29	5th Infantry Division	2-19-1962	12-15-1970
	4th Infantry Division	12-15-1970	12-15-1989
B-29	Fort Benning Georgia	6-21-1958	3-24-1964
	Fort Sill Oklahoma	6-25-1965	10-30-1965

64

	41st Artillery Group	10-30-1965	6-23-1972
2-29	8th Infantry Division	4-1-1984	1-17-1992
	1st Armored Division	1-17-1992	8-16-1995
C-29	Westminister Maryland	6-1-1959	9-16-1979
3-29	4th Infantry Division	4-1-1984	Present
D-29	Las Vegas Nevada	1-23-1963	11-16-1981
4-29	8th Infantry Division	4-1-1984	1-17-1992
	1st Armored Division	1-17-1992	2-15-1997
E-29	Rushville Indiana	5-1-1959	3-15-1976
5-29	4th Infantry Division	4-1-1984	1-16-1996
F-29	1st Armored Division	9-21-1978	4-1-1984
6-29	4th Infantry Division	5-6-1959	12-15-1970
	8th Infantry Division	4-1-1984	1-17-1992
	1st Armored Division	1-17-1992	2-15-1997
G-29	Fort Sill Oklahoma	10-5-1966	3-24-1967
	24th Corps Artillery	3-24-1967	10-1-1971
	2nd Armored Division	12-21-1977	- -1986
H-29	Fort Sill Oklahoma	10-5-1966	3-24-1967
	9th Infantry Division	3-24-1967	10-1967
	2nd F. F. Artillery	10-1967	3-31-1972
	4th Infantry Division	6-21-1976	6-16-1986
I-29	Fort Sill Oklahoma	10-5-1966	3-24-1967
	2nd F. F. Artillery	3-24-1967	4-30-1971
	1st Cavalry Division	6-21-1976	1-22-1977
K-29	Fort Bragg North Carolina	5-25-1967	8-26-1968
	5th Infantry Division	9-30-1978	3-16-1987

30th Field Artillery Regiment-Active Component

1-30	Fort Lewis Washington	6-25-1958	--------------
	Fort Sill Oklahoma	--------------	11-28-1965
	52nd Artillery Group	11-28-1965	2-10-1968
	1st Cavalry Division	2-10-1968	4-7-1971
	Fort Sill Oklahoma	4-7-1971	5-18-1988
	USAFAS-Fort Sill Oklahoma (T)	7-1-1995	12-7-2006
	428th Field Artillery Brigade	12-7-2006	Present
2-30	Fort Bliss Texas	6-25-1958	--------------
	Fort Sill Oklahoma	--------------	10-25-1968
	Italy	9-13-1972	12-12-1975
	USAFATC-Fort Sill Oklahoma (T)	2-28-1987	- -1992

3-30	Fort Sill Oklahoma	6-25-1958	----------------
	Germany	--------------	----------------
	Fort Sill Oklahoma	--------------	6-30-1971
	USAFAS-Fort Sill Oklahoma (T)	7-1-1995	
4-30	Bartlesville Oklahoma	4-1-1959	12-31-1967
D-30	Bartlesville Oklahoma	12-31-1967	3-16-1979
5-30	Fort Sill Oklahoma	4-15-1963	--------------
	Italy	--------------	9-13-1972
	USAFAS-Fort Sill Oklahoma (T)	-1989	- -1990

31st Field Artillery-Active Component

1-31	7th Infantry Division	7-1-1957	2-20-1971
	2nd Infantry Division	2-20-1971	6-17-1979
	USFATC-Fort Sill Oklahoma	2-27-1987	4-15-1996
2-31	Fort Sill Oklahoma	6-25-1958	9-15-1972
	Fort Campbell Kentucky	12-21-1975	- -1989
3-31	102nd Infantry Division	6-1-1959	12-31-1965
4-31	103rd Infantry Division	5-18-1959	3-15-1963
5-31	1st Cavalry Division	7-1-1960	7-1-1963
6-31	77th Infantry Division	5-1-1959	12-31-1965

32nd Field Artillery Regiment-Active Component

1-32	Germany	7-1-1957	7-16-1987
	41st Field Artillery Brigade	7-16-1987	1-15-1992
2-32	Fort Hood Texas	6-26-1958	3-1-1962
	Fort Sill Oklahoma	1-4-1963	11-3-1965
	23rd Artillery Group	11-3-1965	1-22-1972
	Fort Lewis Washington	1-22-1972	7-31-1972
	41st Field Artillery Brigade	8-16-1987	9-15-2004
3-32	Fort Sill Oklahoma	8-1-1957	8-25-1972
	41st Field Artillery Brigade	8-16-1987	1-15-1992
4-32	Tulsa Oklahoma	4-1-1959	2-23-1963
5-32	1st Infantry Division	4-20-1960	3-16-1969
	1st Infantry Division	4-10-1974	5-21-1974
6-32	Fort Lewis Washington	7-10-1962	3-21-1967
	41st Artillery Group	3-21-1967	11-2-1971
	Fort Sill Oklahoma	11-2-1971	7-31-1972
	212th Field Artillery Brigade	8-16-1987	11-16-2006

66

33rd Field Artillery Regiment-Active Component

1-33	Germany	7-1-1957	3-31-1974
	USAFATC-Fort Sill Oklahoma (T)	2-28-1987	8-15-1995
	1st Infantry Division	9-16-1999	6-8-2006
A-33	1st Infantry Division	2-16-1996	9-16-1999
2-33	1st Infantry Division	4-4-1960	9-16-1999
3-33	Wilmington Delaware	6-1-1959	2-28-1963
B-3-33	Fort Miles Delaware		3-28-1963
4-33	Baltimore Maryland	6-1-1959	12-20-1965
5-33	Fort Sill Oklahoma	3-26-1960	6-21-1961
6-33	Fort Carson Colorado	9-1-1967	2-20-1968
	108th Artillery Group	2-20-1968	2-28-1970
	Fort Sill Oklahoma	11-21-1975	8-16-1987
	Camp Mercer Korea		8-16-1987

34th Field Artillery Regiment-Active Component

1-34	9th Infantry Division	12-1-1957	7-1-1958
	24th Infantry Division	7-1-1958	4-15-1970
2-34	Germany	6-25-1958	--------------
	Fort Lewis Washington	--------------	--------------
	75th Field Artillery Brigade	--------------	9-15-1989
3-34	103rd Infantry Division	5-18-1959	3-15-1963
	9th Infantry Division	2-1-1966	8-1-1969
	9th Infantry Division	10-21-1972	10-2-1986
4-34	102nd Infantry Division	6-1-1959	12-31-1965
5-34	96th Infantry Division	6-1-1959	4-15-1963

35th Field Artillery Regiment-Active Component

1-35	24th Infantry Division	4-1-1960	4-15-1970
	24th Infantry Division	6-21-1975	8-16-1986
2-35	Fort Lewis Washington	6-25-1958	--------------
	Fort Carson Colorado	--------------	6-17-1966
	23rd-54th Artillery Groups	6-17-1966	3-31-1971
	Fort Sill Oklahoma	3-31-1971	5-31-1971
	24th Infantry Division	6-21-1977	8-16-1986
3-35	Germany	6-25-1958	--------------
	72nd Field Artillery Brigade	--------------	- -1991
	3rd Infantry Division	- -1991	4-15-1992

4-36	96th Infantry Division	6-1-1959	3-15-1963
	Billings Montana	3-15-1963	2-28-1968
5-35	63rd Infantry Division	6-1-1959	4-1-1963

36th Field Artillery Regiment-Active Component

1-36	Fort Sill Oklahoma	6-25-1958	--------------
	17th Field Artillery Brigade	--------------	- -1991
2-36	Fort Sill Oklahoma	6-1-1958	9-13-1972
	Fort Sill Oklahoma	3-1-1976	- -1986
3-36	Hampton Virginia	6-1-1959	1-31-1968
4-36	Akron Ohio	6-1-1959	1-31-1968

37th Field Artillery Regiment-Active Component

1-37	Fort Richardson Alaska	6-20-1957	12-16-1957
	Fort Richardson Alaska	6-1-1960	5-20-1963
	172nd Infantry Brigade	5-20-1963	4-15-1986
	6th Infantry Division	4-15-1986	10-2-1986
	2nd Infantry Division	4-16-1995	Present
A-37	Fort Richardson Alaska	12-16-1957	6-1-1960
2-37	Fort Sill Oklahoma	6-25-1958	- -1987
3-37	Germany	6-25-1958	- -1986
4-37	Clarksburg West Virginia	6-1-1959	1-31-1968
5-37	79th Infantry Division	4-6-1959	2-28-1963
6-37	2nd Infantry Division	5-2-1960	11-30-2006
	210th Fires Brigade	11-30-2006	Present

38th Field Artillery Regiment-Active Component

1-38	Germany	6-25-1958	10-20-1963
	2nd Infantry Division	9-13-1972	10-1-1983
	2nd Infantry Division	4-16-2002	11-30-2006
	210th Fires Brigade	11-30-2006	Present
A-38	2nd Infantry Division	3-15-1993	4-16-2002
2-38	Germany	6-25-1958	2-20-1963
3-38	South Korea	6-25-1958	12-24-1960
	Fort Sill Oklahoma	2-6-1962	9-30-1974
4-38	Saginaw Michigan	5-1-1959	4-1-1960
	Bay City Michigan	4-1-1960	9-1-1993
5-38	2nd Infantry Division	5-2-1960	9-13-1972

39th Field Artillery Regiment-Active Component

1-39	Germany	6-25-1958	4-15-1964
	108th Artillery Group	10-10-1969	12-21-1971
	18th Field Artillery Brigade	9-13-1972	1-15-1996
	3rd Infantry Division	6-14-2000	Present
A-39	3rd Infantry Division	2-16-1996	6-14-2000
2-39	Fort Sill Oklahoma	6-25-1958	9-25-1958
	3rd Infantry Division	4-1-1960	8-16-1986
3-39	Germany	6-25-1958	12-20-1963
4-39	Pontiac Michigan	9-1-1959	12-31-1965
	Fort Bragg North Carolina	3-25-1967	9-13-1972
5-39	Fort Sill Oklahoma	2-20-1960	--------------
	Germany	--------------	10-25-1963

40th Field Artillery-Active Component

1-40	Fort Bliss Texas	6-25-1958	4-24-1963
	Fort Sill Oklahoma	2-21-1966	10-18-1966
	108th Artillery Group	10-18-1966	11-20-1969
	3rd Armored Division	9-13-1972	9-16-1987
	USAFATC-Fort Sill Oklahoma	1-15-1996	Present
A-40	3rd Armored Division	9-16-1987	1-15-1992
2-40	Germany	6-25-1958	12-15-1963
	199th Infantry Brigade	6-1-1966	10-15-1970
3-40	Syracuse New York	8-15-1959	1-31-1968
4-40	Waterbury New York	9-1-1959	12-23-1965
5-40	Fort Sill Oklahoma	1-23-1960	11-1-1963
6-40	3rd Armored Division	9-1-1963	9-13-1972

41st Field Artillery Regiment-Active Component

1-41	Germany	7-1-1957	6-25-1963
	Germany	9-13-1972	1-17-1986
	24th Infantry Division	8-16-1988	2-15-1996
	3rd Infantry Division	2-15-1996	Present
2-41	3rd Infantry Division	4-1-1960	5-16-1992
3-41	Brooklyn New York	8-8-1959	--------------
	Fort Tilden New York	------------	12-30-1965
	24th Infantry Division	8-16-1988	2-15-1996

4-41	Fort Sill Oklahoma	4-20-1960	4-24-1961
	Fort Sill Oklahoma	1-14-1963	--------------
	Germany	--------------	9-13-1972
	197th Infantry Brigade	8-16-1988	6-14-1991
	24th Infantry Division	6-14-1991	2-15-1996
5-41	Fort Sill Oklahoma	5-22-1959	11-1-1963
	3rd Infantry Division	8-16-1988	2-15-1996
E-41	Fort Sill Oklahoma	6-25-1966	3-24-1967
	1st F.F. Artillery	3-24-1967	12-26-1971
6-41	3rd Infantry Division	8-16-1988	5-16-1992

42nd Field Artillery-Active Component

1-42	Germany	4-18-1959	9-30-1977
2-42	Fort Bragg North Carolina	6-21-1958	2-1-1963
	11th Air Assault Division	2-1-1963	6-30-1965
	Fort Benning Georgia	6-30-1965	4-1-1968
	Germany	10-1-1973	- -1987
3-42	Newark New Jersey	8-1-1959	--------------
	Jersey City New Jersey	--------------	9-1-1993
	Pennsylvania	9-1-1993	9-1-1995
4-42	4th Infantry Division	5-6-1959	12-15-1970
	4th Infantry Division	1-16-1996	Present
	17th Field Artillery Brigade	7-16-1987	3-1-1991
5-42	Fort Sill Oklahoma	6-20-1959	--------------
	Germany	--------------	10-25-1963
	Fort Bragg North Carolina	1-25-1967	4-2-1968
	23rd Artillery Group	4-2-1968	4-1-1972
	Fort Lewis Washington	4-1-1972	7-31-1972

43rd Air Defense Artillery Regiment-Active Component

1-43	Fairchild AFB Washington	9-1-1958	3-25-1966
	Fort Richardson Alaska	9-13-1972	7-31-1979
	Fort Bliss Texas	5-1-1982	Present
2-43	Redmond Washington	9-1-1958	--------------
	Turner AFB Georgia	--------------	3-25-1966
	108th ADA Brigade	1-1-1984	Present
3-43	Lumberton New Jersey	9-1-1958	--------------
	Pedricktown New Jersey	--------------	9-15-1974
	11th ADA Brigade	7-1-1987	

70

4-43	Fort Richardson Alaska	9-1-1958	9-13-1972
	11th ADA Brigade	3-16-1989	5-2-1996
5-43	Glassmare Pennsylvania FA	6-1-1959	--------------
	New Kingston Pennsylvania FA	------------	1-31-1968
6-43	Omaha AFB Nebraska	6-24-1960	6-25-1966
	69th ADA Brigade	3-16-1989	2-15-1996
8-43	69th ADA Brigade	3-16-1989	12-15-1991
16D-43	Fort Lewis Washington	9-1-1958	7-2-1962

44th Air Defense Artillery Regiment-Active Component

1-44	Germany	9-1-1958	8-10-1960
	Fort Bliss Texas	3-1-1966	--------------
	South Korea	------------	6-30-1980
	9th Infantry Division	3-16-1988	2-16-1991
	4th Infantry Division	1-16-1996	12-16-2004
	11th ADA Brigade	12-16-2004	Present
2-44	Fort Lewis Washington	3-31-1958	7-20-1960
	Fort Sill Oklahoma	6-23-1962	9-1-1971
	South Korea	9-13-1972	9-30-1977
	101st Airborne Division	3-16-1988	
3-44	Fairchild Connecticut	9-1-1958	7-20-1960
	94th ADA Brigade	3-16-1988	7-15-1991
4-44	Fort Bliss Texas	9-1-1958	--------------
	South Korea	------------	9-13-1972
5-44	Schilling AFB Kansas	4-18-1960	6-26-1960
	108th ADA Brigade	3-16-1988	7-15-1991
E-44	199th Infantry Brigade	2-16-1991	7-16-1992
	Fort Lewis Washington	7-16-1992	2-15-1994
6-44	Fort Bliss Texas	7-1-1962	--------------
	South Korea	------------	9-13-1972
12D-44	Waterbury Connecticut	2-1-1960	3-1-1963
16D-44	Fort Bliss Texas	9-1-1958	3-12-1959

49th Field Artillery Regiment-National Guard

1-49	115th Artillery Group	8-1-1959	------------
	115th Field Artillery Brigade	------------	9-1-1996
2-49	115th Artillery Group	8-1-1959	12-18-1967
3-49	115th Artillery Group	8-1-1959	------------
	115th Field Artillery Brigade	------------	9-1-1989
	163rd Armored Brigade	9-1-1989	9-1-1996

51st Air Defense Artillery Regiment-Active Component

1-51	Plainview Connecticut	9-1-1958	3-25-1961
	Highlands New Jersey	9-13-1972	6-4-1973
	7th Infantry Division	12-21-1975	8-16-1986
2-51	San Francisco California	9-1-1958	-------------
	Fort Baker California	------------	9-13-1972
3-51	Fort Tilden New York	9-1-1958	-------------
	Highlands New Jersey	------------	9-13-1972
4-51	Fort Monroe Virginia	9-1-1958	7-20-1960
5-51	Fort Tilden New York (FA)	8-8-1959	9-1-1971
6-51	Mountain Home AFB Idaho	9-1-1958	7-26-1960

52nd Air Defense Artillery Regiment-Active Component

1-52	Camp Hanford Washington	9-1-1958	12-23-1960
	35th ADA Brigade	4-16-1988	4-15-1993
2-52	Fort Bliss Texas	4-15-1959	4-15-1988
	108th ADA Brigade	4-16-1988	
3-52	Squantum Massachusetts	9-1-1958	-------------
	Quincy Massachusetts	------------	12-15-1961
	10th ADA Brigade	4-16-1988	4-15-1992
4-52	Chicago Illinois	9-1-1958	6-24-1960
5-52	24th Infantry Division	12-21-1975	11-16-1988
	11th ADA Brigade	9-16-1996	Present
6-52	Fort Bliss Texas	11-17-1960	------------
	69th ADA Brigade	4-16-1988	9-15-1993
	69th ADA Brigade	2-15-1996	9-18-2006
	214th Fires Brigade	9-18-2006	Present

55th Air Defense Artillery Regiment-Active Component

1-55	Fort Totten New York	9-1-1958	7-26-1960
	5th Infantry Division	12-21-1975	7-16-1989
2-55	Manchester Connecticut	9-1-1958	-------------
	New Britain Connecticut	------------	12-24-1964
	Fort Bliss Texas	9-13-1972	
3-55	Fort Wayne Michigan	9-1-1958	----------------
	Kerchival Michigan	------------	12-23-1960
4-55	Thule Greenland	9-1-1958	----------------

	Fort Totten New York	------------	12-20-1960
5-55	Kansas City Kansas	9-1-1959	----------------
	Olathe NAS Kansas	------------	2-10-1969
F-55	Fort Bliss Texas	4-22-1960	----------------
	Fort Amador Canal Zone	--------------	9-10-1960
G-55	Fort Bliss Texas	10-14-1966	1-20-1967
	Fort Bliss Texas	8-1-1967	--------------
	South Vietnam	------------	7-31-1971
12P-55	Fort Benning Georgia	6-20-1958	9-23-1960
16D-55	Fort Stewart Georgia	9-1-1958	11-12-1963

56th Air Defense Artillery Regiment-Active Component

1-56	Pasadena California	9-1-1958	----------------
	Saugus California	------------	12-12-1968
	Fort Bliss Texas (T)	3-16-1988	Present
2-56	Germany	9-1-1958	
	Fort Bliss Texas (T)	3-16-1988	
3-56	West Haven Connecticut	9-1-1958	9-1-1961
	Fort Bliss Texas (T)	3-16-1988	
C-56	Fort Bliss Texas	6-30-1971	12-20-1971
4-56	Bristol Rhode Island	9-1-1958	--------------
	Reoboth Massachusetts	------------	8-26-1963
	Fort Bliss Texas	5-20-1967	3-31-1970
	Fort Bliss Texas (T)	3-16-1988	
5-56	Cincinnati Ohio	6-15-1959	--------------
	Wilmington Ohio	--------------	3-31-1970
6-56	Fort Bliss Texas	7-25-1962	9-30-1965
	97th Artillery Group	10-30-1965	8-2-1969
	Fort Bliss Texas	8-2-1969	8-10-1969
	Germany	9-13-1972	3-16-1988
16D-56	Camp Wellfleet Massachusetts	9-1-1958	6-25-1961

57th Air Defense Artillery Regiment-Active Component

1-57	Boston Massachusetts	9-1-1958	--------------
	Nahant Massachusetts	------------	6-25-1960
	Fort Sill Oklahoma	3-25-1961	--------------
	Okinawa	--------------	12-1-1968
	Fort Bliss Texas	8-16-1971	3-19-1973

2-57	Chicago Illinois	9-1-1958	8-23-1963
	Germany	9-13-1972	
3-57	Los Angeles California	9-1-1958	--------------
	Fort MacArthur California	------------	4-24-1964
4-57	Germany	9-1-1958	9-13-1972
5-57	Fort Bliss Texas	6-1-1959	
6-57	Fort Bliss Texas	10-25-1967	7-25-1968

59th Air Defense Artillery-Active Component

1-59	Fort Bliss Texas	9-1-1958	5-26-1960
	Fort Bliss Texas	5-5-1969	11-4-1969
	8th Infantry Division	11-4-1969	7-16-1989
B-1-59	Fort Bliss Texas	5-26-1960	3-26-1963
2-59	Edgemont Pennsylvania	9-1-1958	10-9-1964
	Fort Bliss Texas	5-1-1970	11-4-1970
	4th Armored Division	11-4-1970	5-10-1971
	1st Armored Division	5-10-1971	7-16-1989
3-59	Milwaukee Wisconsin	9-1-1958	6-30-1971
	Germany	9-13-1972	
4-59	Norfolk Virginia (HHC)	9-1-1958	6-30-1971
	Norfolk Virginia (BA-B-C)	9-1-1958	3-30-1971
5-59	Fort Bliss Texas	1-11-1971	9-30-1974
6-59	Fort Bliss Texas	11-17-1960	--------------
	Germany	----------------	9-13-1972
12P-59	Fort Bliss Texas	9-1-1958	9-12-1960
16D-59	Fort Bliss Texas	9-1-1958	9-17-1962

60th Air Defense Artillery Regiment-Active Component

1-60	Gary Indiana	9-1-1958	--------------
	Munster Indiana	------------	9-30-1974
2-60	Orland Park Illinois	9-1-1958	12-15-1961
	Fort Bliss Texas	1-12-1970	3-16-1988
3-60	Eureka Pennsylvania	9-1-1958	9-1-1961
	Germany	9-13-1972	
4-60	Midway Washington	9-1-1958	--------------
	Redmond Washington	------------	12-15-1961
	Fort Bliss Texas	6-25-1966	--------------
	41st Artillery Group	--------------	--------------
	Germany	--------------	7-3-1972

5-60	South Bend Indiana (FA)	9-1-1959	9-1-1971
6-60	Fort Bliss Texas	3-25-1961	------------
	Germany	--------------	9-13-1972
7-60	Fort Bliss Texas	6-20-1970	12-11-1970
	82nd Airborne Division	12-11-1970	9-13-1972
12P-60	Ladd AFB Alaska	9-1-1958	9-15-1960
16D-60	Fort Bliss Texas	9-1-1958	7-1-1962

61st Air Defense Artillery Regiment-Active Component

1-61	Travis AFB California	9-1-1958	8-30-1974
2-61	Okinawa	9-1-1958	5-1-1970
	2nd Infantry Division	9-13-1972	11-16-1988
3-61	Loring AFB Maine	9-1-1958	6-25-1966
	Fort Bliss Texas	3-9-1970	9-2-1970
	3rd Armored Division	9-2-1970	11-16-1988
4-61	Fort Winfield Scott California	9-1-1958	--------------
	Robbins AFB Georgia	------------	3-25-1960
	Fort Bliss Texas	1-3-1969	8-14-1969
	5th Infantry Division	8-14-1969	12-15-1970
	4th Infantry Division	12-15-1970	7-16-1989
5-61	Fort Bliss Texas	9-1-1958	4-22-1959
6-61	Fort Bliss Texas	4-25-1961	9-13-1972
7-61	Fort Bliss Texas	11-10-1969	--------------
	Germany	--------------	9-13-1972
8-61	Fort Bliss Texas	9-6-1970	9-1-1971
	2nd Infantry Division	9-1-1971	9-13-1972
12D-61	Lafayette Indiana	9-1-1959	1-31-1961
16D-61	Camp Haven Wisconsin	9-1-1958	7-1-1962

62nd Air Defense Artillery Regiment-Active Component

1-62	St. Louis Missouri	6-1-1959	--------------
	Scott AFB Illinois	------------	1-15-1969
	Fort Bliss Texas	3-15-1971	1-6-1972
	25th Infantry Division	1-6-1972	9-16-2005
2-62	Lancaster New York	9-1-1958	12-15-1961
	Germany	9-13-1972	
	7th Infantry Division	8-16-1986	9-15-1993
3-62	Fort Bragg North Carolina	3-1-1958	9-25-1961
	Fort Bliss Texas	2-1-1966	--------------
	10th Infantry Division	------------	- -2005

4-62	Fort MacArthur California	9-1-1958	--------------
	Fort Bliss Texas	------------	9-30-1979
	6th Infantry Division	8-16-1986	7-6-1994
5-62	11th ADA Brigade	8-16-1986	10-15-1992
6-62	Fort Bliss Texas	4-19-1962	--------------
	Germany	--------------	9-13-1972
12D-62	Elmendorf AFB Alaska	9-1-1958	9-15-1960
16D-62	Fort Bliss Texas	9-1-1958	9-23-1962

65th Air Defense Artillery Regiment-Active Component

1-65	Okinawa	9-1-1958	5-1-1970
	Key West Florida	9-13-1972	9-30-1974
2-65	Camp Kilmer New Jersey	9-1-1958	7-26-1960
	Van Nuys California	9-13-1972	9-30-1974
3-65	Cleveland Ohio	9-1-1958	6-30-1971
4-65	Los Angeles California	9-1-1958	--------------
	Van Nuys California	------------	9-13-1972
6-65	Fort Bliss Texas	12-15-1961	--------------
	Key West Florida	--------------	9-13-1972
G-65	Fort Bliss Texas	3-1-1966	--------------
	South Vietnam	------------	12-26-1971
12D-65	Clarion Pennsylvania	6-1-1959	2-11-1963
16D-65	Camp Irwin California	9-1-1958	7-2-1962

67th Air Defense Artillery Regiment-Active Component

1-67	Germany	9-1-1958	12-26-2969
	9th Infantry Division	11-21-1972	3-16-1988
2-67	Ellsworth AFB South Korea	9-1-1958	8-25-1961
	1st Infantry Division	9-13-1972	7-16-1989
3-67	Milwaukee Wisconsin	9-1-1958	8-25-1961
	3rd Infantry Division	9-13-1972	7-16-1989
4-67	San Pablo California	9-1-1958	6-28-1968
5-67	Fort Bliss Texas	8-1-1968	9-13-1972
6-67	Fort Bliss Texas	4-22-1960	--------------
	Fort Amador Canal Zone	--------------	9-10-1960
	Fort Bliss Texas	10-7-1968	6-30-1969
	24th Infantry Division	6-30-1969	4-15-1970
	1st Infantry Division	4-15-1970	9-13-1972

7-67	Fort Bliss Texas	7-7-1959	3-3-1970
	3rd Infantry Division	3-3-1970	9-13-1972
16D-67	Erie ORD Department Ohio	9-1-1959	--------------
	Fort Knox Kentucky	------------	5-10-1963

68th Air Defense Artillery Regiment-Active Component

1-68	Cleveland Ohio	9-1-1958	8-25-1961
	Fort Sill Oklahoma	8-15-1963	--------------
	Germany	--------------	6-23-1970
	1st Cavalry Division	9-13-1972	11-16-1988
2-68	Camp Lacus	9-1-1958	6-15-1960
3-68	Germany	9-1-1958	11-20-1958
	Minneapolis Minnesota	6-1-1959	--------------
	Fort Snelling Minnesota	------------	6-30-1971
4-68	Coventry Rhode Island	9-1-1958	12-15-1961
6-68	Fort Bliss Texas	5-10-1971	7-5-1972
	1st Cavalry Division	7-5-1972	9-13-1972
G-68	Fort Bliss Texas	2-1-1966	12-27-1971
16D-68	Camp Lucas Michigan	9-1-1958	6-1-1960

69th Air Defense Artillery Regiment-National Guard

1-69	42nd Infantry Division	9-1-1993	9-1-1996

70th Air Defense Artillery Regiment-National Guard

1-70	691st Artillery Group (AD)	3-1-1959	1-1-1968
	Granite Maryland	1-1-1968	9-30-1974
2-70	691st Artillery Group (AD)	3-1-1959	1-1-1968
3-70	691st Artillery Group (AD)	3-1-1959	1-1-1968

71st Air Defense Artillery Regiment-Active Component

1-71	Suitland Maryland	9-1-1958	- -1965
2-71	Taiwan	9-1-1958	8-15-1959
	Fort Bliss Texas	3-1-1960	--------------
	South Korea	------------	7-20-1962
3-71	Germany	9-1-1958	
4-71	Fort Hancock New Jersey	9-1-1958	6-19-1964

D-71	Fort Bliss Texas	6-1-1967	--------------
	South Vietnam	------------	6-25-1971
	South Vietnam	9-15-1971	2-20-1972
6-71	Fort Bliss Texas	6-6-1962	--------------
	97th Artillery Group	------------	3-30-1970
16D-71	Fort Bliss Texas	9-1-1958	9-17-1962

73rd Field Artillery Regiment-Active Component

1-73	1st Armored Division	2-15-1957	5-5-1971
	Fort Bragg North Carolina	5-5-1971	10-1-1983
2-73	3rd Armored Division	10-1-1957	6-17-1974
3-73	77th Infantry Division	5-1-1959	3-26-1963
	Fort Irwin California	1-1-1967	7-21-1972
4-73	94th Infantry Division	5-1-1959	3-1-1963
	Fort Bragg North Carolina	2-25-1967	5-28-1971
5-73	Fort Sill Oklahoma	1-3-1963	--------------
	Germany	------------	9-30-1973

75th Field Artillery Regiment-Active Component

1-75	Germany	6-25-1958	5-16-1988
2-75	Germany	6-25-1958	3-16-1989
3-75	Springfield Illinois	10-1-1959	9-1-1995
4-75	Chicago Illinois	10-1-1959	12-31-1965
	Peoria Illinois	12-31-1965	9-1-1993
F-75	Fort Benning Georgia	11-2-1965	11-16-1965
G-75	Fort Stewart Georgia	7-25-1967	6-30-1971

76th Field Artillery Regiment-Active Component

1-76	2nd Infantry Brigade	2-15-1958	3-25-1962
	3rd Infantry Division	9-13-1972	3-16-1987
	3rd Infantry Division	6-24-2004	Present
A-76	3rd Infantry Division	3-16-1987	2-16-1996
2-76	South Korea	6-25-1958	--------------
	Fort Lewis Washington	--------------	6-27-1971
	Fort Riley Kansas	12-21-1975	5-17-1978
3-76	Fort Carson Colorado	6-1-1958	9-25-1958
	3rd Infantry Division	4-1-1960	9-13-1972

4-76	7th Infantry Division	7-1-1960	4-2-1971
5-76	Winooski Vermont	9-1-1959	-----------------
	Burlington Vermont	------------	12-22-1965

77th Field Artillery Regiment-Active Component

1-77	Germany	6-25-1958	6-25-1959
	1st Cavalry Division	7-1-1960	6-16-1986
	194th Armored Brigade	8-17-1986	9-16-1990
	75th Field Artillery Brigade	4-16-1996	Present
A-77	194th Armored Brigade	9-16-1990	9-16-1995
2-77	Fort Hood Texas	8-1-1957	1-2-1959
	4th Infantry Division	5-6-1959	8-1-1967
	25th Infantry Division	8-1-1967	12-15-1970
	17th Field Artillery Brigade	5-16-1988	3-1-1991
	4th Infantry Division	12-16-2004	Present
3-77	63rd Infantry Division	6-1-1959	12-31-1965
4-77	90th Infantry Division	4-1-1959	3-15-1963
	101st Airborne Division	9-1-1968	1-21-1978
	41st Field Artillery Brigade	3-25-1983	3-1-1991
5-77	Fort Sill Oklahoma	9-12-1962	--------------
	Germany	--------------	6-30-1971
6-77	Fort Sill Oklahoma	10-15-1966	5-12-1967
	54th Artillery Group	5-12-1967	6-1-1969
F-77	1st Cavalry Division	4-30-1971	8-12-1971

78th Field Artillery Regiment-Active Component

1-78	2nd Armored Division	7-1-1957 T	10-1-1983
	USAFATC-Fort Sill Oklahoma	2-27-1987	12-7-2006
	428th Field Artillery Brigade	12-7-2006	12-7-2006
2-78	4th Armored Division	4-1-1957	5-10-1971
	1st Armored Division	5-10-1971	1-16-1988
3-78	90th Infantry Division	4-1-1959	12-31-1965
4-78	102nd Infantry Division	6-1-1959	12-31-1965
E-78	194th Armored Brigade	12-21-1962	5-14-1964
	Fort Ord California	1-4-1968	5-18-1970
5-78	194th Armored Brigade	5-14-1964	1-4-1968
6-78	6th Infantry Division	11-24-1967	7-24-1968

79th Field Artillery Regiment-Active Component

1-79	Italy	6-24-1958	6-25-1959
	7th Infantry Division	7-1-1960	4-2-1971
	7th Infantry Division	10-21-1975	10-1-1983
	USAFATC-Fort Sill Oklahoma (T)	8-16-1995	Present
2-79	Fort Hood Texas	6-25-1958	--------------
	Fort Carson Colorado	--------------	2-19-1962
	Fort Sill Oklahoma	4-14-1964	11-30-1968
3-79	Fort Hood Texas	8-1-1957	--------------
	Germany	--------------	
4-79	Ada Oklahoma	4-1-1959	12-31-1965
5-79	St. Petersburg Florida	5-15-1959	12-31-1965
F-79	1st Cavalry Division	6-30-1971	8-22-1972
	1st Cavalry Division	3-24-1974	12-20-1974

80th Field Artillery Regiment-Active Component

1-80	Italy	6-25-1958	11-25-1963
	6th Infantry Division	11-24-1967	7-25-1968
	Germany	11-1-1974	7-16-1987
2-80	Fort Sill Oklahoma	6-25-1958	3-25-1963
	USAFATC-Fort Sill Oklahoma (T)	2-27-1987	Present
3-80	Germany	6-25-1958	1-9-1963
	Fort Sill Oklahoma	4-15-1963	--------------
	Germany	--------------	6-23-1970
4-80	Peoria Illinois	6-1-1959	12-31-1965
	Fort Carson Colorado	3-1-1967	2-26-1971
5-80	5th Infantry Division	11-15-1969	12-15-1970
6-80	7th Infantry Division	7-1-1960	4-2-1971
	7th Infantry Division	11-21-1975	10-1-1983

81st Field Artillery Regiment-Active Component

1-81	Fort Hood Texas	6-25-1958	--------------
	Fort Carson Colorado	--------------	8-25-1961
	Fort Sill Oklahoma	4-15-1963	--------------
	Germany	--------------	1-17-1986
2-81	Germany	6-25-1958	10-15-1963
	8th Infantry Division	8-31-1973	4-1-1984

80

3-81	Germany	6-25-1958	6-18-1960
	Fort Sill Oklahoma	6-22-1962	--------------
	South Korea	--------------	5-29-1977
4-81	Jonesboro Arkansas	4-1-1959	12-31-1965
5-81	8th Infantry Division	5-1-1960	8-31-1973
6-81	11th Air Assault Division	7-18-1963	7-1-1965

82nd Field Artillery Regiment-Active Component

1-82	Italy	6-24-1958	4-20-1964
	23rd Infantry Division	1-10-1968	4-30-1971
	Fort Bragg North Carolina	11-30-1971	6-21-1975
	1st Cavalry Division	6-21-1975	Present
2-82	Germany	6-25-1958	3-25-1964
	3rd Armored Division	6-16-1988	9-15-1991
	1st Cavalry Division	12-16-1992	Present
3-82	Germany	6-25-1958	12-20-1963
	196th Infantry Brigade	9-15-1965	2-15-1969
	23rd Infantry Division	2-15-1969	11-1-1971
	196th Infantry Brigade	11-1-1971	6-30-1972
	1st Cavalry Division	6-16-1986	Present
4-82	Tuscaloosa Alabama	6-1-1959	1-31-1968
	3rd Armored Division	6-16-1986	9-15-1991
	42nd Field Artillery Brigade	9-15-1991	6-30-1995
5-82	1st Cavalry Division	7-1-1960	7-1-1965
	1st Cavalry Division	10-17-2005	Present
E-82	1st Cavalry Division	7-1-1965	4-10-1971
	1st Cavalry Division	1-21-1977	8-16-1987
6-82	Fort Bragg North Carolina	6-1-1967	11-30-1971

83rd Field Artillery Regiment-Active Component

1-83	Fort Bragg North Carolina	6-1-1958	------------------
	Fort Sill Oklahoma	-------------	10-30-1968
	54th-108th Artillery Groups	10-30-1968	6-7-1971
	8th Infantry Division	9-13-1972	4-1-1984
2-83	Germany	6-1-1958	7-16-1988
3-83	Laurel Mississippi	6-1-1959	9-1-1995
4-83	Charlestown West Virginia	5-1-1959	1-31-1968
5-83	8th Infantry Division	5-1-1960	9-13-1972
6-83	Ogden Utah	2-15-1963	9-1-1991

84th Field Artillery Regiment-Active Component

1-84	Fort Sill Oklahoma	6-25-1958	4-19-1962
	9th Infantry Division	2-1-1966	9-25-1969
	9th Infantry Division	10-21-1972	8-15-1988
A-84	Fort Knox Kentucky	- -1995	- -1997
2-84	Germany	6-25-1958	1-25-1964
	Fort Carson Colorado	5-26-1967	2-26-1971
3-84	Germany	6-25-1958	6-18-1960
	Fort Sill Oklahoma	2-1-1964	--------------
	Germany	------------	1-17-1986
4-84	Columbus Ohio	10-1-1959	12-31-1965
	Fort Carson Colorado	2-23-1967	2-26-1971
5-84	South Bend Indiana	5-1-1959	1-31-1968
6-84	Fort Irwin California	8-25-1967	3-24-1968
	41st-54th Artillery Groups	3-24-1968	8-7-1969

86th Field Artillery Regiment-Active Component

1-86	86th Armored Brigade	2-1-1964	2-1-1968
	50th Armored Division	2-1-1968	6-1-1975
	Williston Vermont	6-1-1975	5-1-1980
	50th Armored Division	5-1-1980	2-1-1988
	26th Infantry Division	2-1-1988	9-1-1993
	Williston Vermont	9-1-1993	
	42nd Infantry Division		

92nd Field Artillery Regiment-Active Component

1-92	Germany	6-25-1958	-------------
	52nd Artillery Group	--------------	-------------
	Fort Bragg North Carolina	--------------	11-20-1971
	2nd Armored Division	11-20-1971	7-1-1986
A-92	2nd Armored Division	7-1-1986	9-16-1990
	1st Cavalry Division	9-16-1990	4-16-1991
	2nd Armored Division	12-2-1992	1-16-1996
2-92	Germany	6-25-1958	4-16-1988
3-92	Canton Ohio	6-1-1959	10-26-1969
	Arkon Ohio	10-26-1969	9-1-1995
4-92	Clearfield Pennsylvania	6-1-1959	11-15-1971
	Erie Pennsylvania	11-15-1971	9-1-1994
5-92	24th Infantry Division	9-1-1960	3-1-1963
6-92	2nd Armored Division	7-8-1963	11-30-1971

94th Field Artillery Regiment-Active Component

1-94	4th Armored Division	6-25-1958	5-10-1971
	1st Armored Division	5-10-1971	11-16-1986
	1st Armored Division	9-16-2000	
A-94	1st Armored Division	11-16-1986	1-15-1992
	1st Armored Division	7-16-1995	9-16-2000
2-94	Fort Sill Oklahoma	6-1-1966	10-18-1966
	108th Artillery Group	10-18-1966	4-2-1971
C-94	Berlin Brigade	9-1-1963	10-2-1986
4-94	Fort Lewis Washington	8-10-1967	--------------
	Fort Irwin California	-------------	3-31-1970
D-94	Fort Knox Kentucky	6-30-1971	12-12-1975

101st Field Artillery Regiment-National Guard

1-101	26th Infantry Division	5-1-1959	9-1-1993
	42nd Infantry Division	9-1-1993	9-1-2003
	29th Infantry Division	9-1-2003	
	42nd Infantry Division		
2-101	26th Infantry Division	5-1-1959	12-19-1967
3-101	26th Infantry Division	5-1-1959	11-1-1974
E-101	42nd Infantry Division	9-1-1993	

102nd Field Artillery Regiment-National Guard

1-102	26th Infantry Division	5-1-1959	9-1-1988
	113th Field Artillery Brigade	10-1-1997	6-15-2002
2-102	26th Infantry Division	5-1-1959	4-1-1975
3-102	26th Infantry Division	5-1-1959	4-1-1963
E-102	26th Infantry Division	10-1-1977	9-1-1988

103rd Field Artillery Regiment-National Guard

1-103	43rd Infantry Division	4-1-1959	3-18-1963
	43rd Corps Artillery	3-18-1963	5-1-1968
	103rd Artillery Group	5-1-1968	------------
	103rd Field Artillery Brigade	------------	Present

2-103	43rd Infantry Division	4-1-1959	3-18-1963
	43rd Corps Artillery	3-18-1963	5-1-1968
	103rd Artillery Group	5-1-1968	------------
	103rd Field Artillery Brigade	------------	9-1-1991
3-103	43rd Infantry Division	4-1-1959	3-18-1963
	43rd Corps Artillery	3-18-1963	2-1-1968
4-103	43rd Infantry Division	4-1-1959	3-18-1963
F-103	Hillsgrove Rhode Island	1-1-1965	3-1-1966

104th Field Artillery Regiment-National Guard

1-104	27th Armored Division	3-16-1959	2-1-1968
2-104	42nd Infantry Division	3-16-1959	9-1-1992

105th Field Artillery Regiment-National Guard

1-105	42nd Infantry Division	3-16-1959	9-1-1991
E-105	42nd Infantry Division	9-1-1989	9-1-1991

106th Field Artillery Regiment-National Guard

1-106	27th Armored Division	3-16-1959	2-1-1968
	42nd Infantry Division	2-1-1968	4-1-1975
2-106	209th Artillery Group (AD)	3-16-1959	4-15-1963

107th Field Artillery Regiment-National Guard

1-107	28th Infantry Division	6-1-1959	2-17-1968
	42nd Infantry Division	2-17-1968	4-1-1975
	28th Infantry Division	4-1-1975	Present

108th Field Artillery Regiment-National Guard

1-108	28th Infantry Division	6-1-1959	4-1-1975
	28th Infantry Division	10-1-1975	Present

109th Field Artillery Regiment-National Guard

1-109	28th Infantry Division	6-1-1959	Present
2-109	28th Infantry Division	6-1-1959	4-1-1963
F-109	28th Infantry Division	10-1-1977	

110th Field Artillery Regiment-National Guard

1-110	29th Infantry Division	5-1-1959	1-21-1968
2-110	29th Infantry Division	5-1-1959	1-21-1968
	28th Infantry Division	1-21-1968	4-1-1975
	58th Infantry Brigade	4-1-1975	7-1-1986
	29th Infantry Division	7-1-1986	Present
3-110	29th Infantry Division	5-1-1959	3-1-1963

111th Field Artillery Regiment-National Guard

1-111	29th Infantry Division	6-1-1959	2-1-1968
	28th Infantry Division	2-1-1968	5-1-1972
	224th Field Artillery Brigade	5-1-1972	6-1-1986
	Norfolk Virginia	6-1-1986	9-1-1991
	29th Infantry Division	10-1-1996	4-1-1998
	54th Field Artillery Brigade	4-1-1998	
	29th Infantry Division		
2-111	Richmond Virginia	3-22-1963	2-1-1968
	224th Artillery Group	2-1-1968	------------
	224th Field Artillery Brigade	------------	6-1-1986
	29th Infantry Division	6-1-1986	4-1-1998
	54th Field Artillery Brigade	4-1-1998	
5-111	107th Artillery Group (AD)	6-1-1959	10-1-1964
	258th Infantry Brigade	10-1-1964	12-10-1967
E-111	29th Infantry Division	6-1-1986	
6-111	224th Artillery Group	3-22-1963	10-1-1964

111th Air Defense Artillery Regiment-National Guard

3-111	107th Artillery Brigade (AD)	6-1-1959	2-1-1968
	107th Artillery Group (AD)	2-1-1968	8-1-1975
	28th Infantry Division	8-1-1975	6-1-1990
	29th Infantry Division	6-1-1990	2-11-2006
4-111	107th Artillery Brigade (AD)	6-1-1959	2-1-1968
	107th Artillery Group (AD)	2-1-1968	9-30-1974
E-111	27th Infantry Brigade	10-1-1999	

112th Field Artillery Regiment-National Guard

1-112	50th Armored Division	3-1-1959	2-1-1968
	112th Artillery Group	2-1-1968	9-1-1975
	50th Armored Division	9-1-1975	9-1-1993
	42nd Infantry Division	9-1-1993	9-1-1997
2-112	50th Armored Division	3-1-1959	1-31-1968
3-112	50th Armored Division	3-1-1959	9-1-1993
	42nd Infantry Division	9-1-1993	Present
4-112	50th Armored Division	3-1-1959	9-1-1991
D-112	42nd Infantry Division	9-1-1997	
5-112	Woodbridge New Jersey	3-1-1959	1-31-1968
	112th Artillery Group	1-31-1968	7-1-1975
	50th Armored Division	7-1-1975	5-1-1980
6-112	Cape May New Jersey	3-1-1959	1-31-1963
	50th Armored Division	1-31-1963	7-1-1975
7-112	New Jersey ADA	3-15-1966	4-1-1972

113th Field Artillery Regiment-National Guard

1-113	30th Infantry Division	4-1-1959	11-30-1973
	30th Infantry Brigade	11-30-1973	9-1-2002
	30th Armored Brigade	9-1-2002	Present
2-113	30th Infantry Division	4-1-1959	1-15-1968
3-113	30th Infantry Division	4-1-1959	1-15-1968
4-113	30th Infantry Division	4-1-1959	1-15-1968
	113th Artillery Group	1-15-1968	--------------
	113th Field Artillery Brigade	--------------	9-1-1996
5-113	30th Infantry Division	4-1-1959	1-15-1968
	113th Artillery Group	1-15-1968	--------------
	113th Field Artillery Brigade	--------------	

114th Field Artillery Regiment-National Guard

1-114	31st Infantry Division	5-2-1959	2-15-1968
	631st Artillery Group	2-15-1968	--------------
	631st Field Artillery Brigade	--------------	
2-114	31st Infantry Division	5-2-1959	2-15-1968
	30th Armored Division	2-15-1968	11-1-1973
	155th Armored Brigade	11-1-1973	
	36th Infantry Division		

86

3-114	31st Infantry Division	5-2-1959	2-15-1968
4-114	631st Artillery Group	5-2-1959	--------------
	631st Field Artillery Brigade	------------	9-1-1994
5-114	631st Artillery Group	5-2-1959	2-15-1968

115th Field Artillery Regiment-National Guard

1-115	30th Armored Division	3-1-1959	11-1-1973
	196th Artillery Group	------------	--------------
	196th Field Artillery Brigade	------------	
2-115	30th Armored Division	3-1-1959	2-1-1968
	196th Field Artillery Brigade	9-1-1996	
3-115	30th Armored Division	3-1-1959	11-1-1973
	30th Armored Brigade	11-1-1973	9-1-1996
	196th Field Artillery Brigade	9-1-1996	
	38th Infantry Division		

116th Field Artillery Regiment-National Guard

1-116	51st Infantry Division	4-15-1959	2-15-1963
	163rd Artillery Group	2-15-1963	3-1-1964
	Sarasota Florida	3-1-1964	1-20-1968
	227th Artillery Group	1-20-1968	--------------
	227th Field Artillery Brigade	--------------	9-1-1993
2-116	48th Armored Division	4-15-1959	2-15-1963
	53rd Infantry Brigade	2-15-1963	3-1-1964
	53rd Armored Brigade	3-1-1964	1-20-1968
	53rd Infantry Brigade	1-20-1968	
	28th Infantry Division		
3-116	51st Infantry Division	4-15-1959	2-15-1963
	163rd Artillery Group	2-15-1963	1-20-1968
	227th Field Artillery Brigade	10-1-1984	9-1-1993
	Plant City Florida	9-1-1993	

117th Field Artillery Regiment-National Guard

1-117	31st Infantry Division	5-1-1959	1-15-1968
	30th Armored Division	1-15-1968	11-1-1973
	31st Armored Brigade	11-1-1973	9-1-2000
	Andalusa Alabama	9-1-2003	

2-117	31st Infantry Division	5-1-1959	1-15-1968
	Huntsville Alabama	4-1-1975	9-1-1992
	Aurburn Alabama	9-1-1997	------------
	631st Field Artillery Brigade	-----------	9-1-2003
	38th Infantry Division		
3-117	Troy Alabama	11-1-1980	------------
	631st Field Artillery Brigade	--------------	

118th Field Artillery Regiment-National Guard

1-118	48th Armored Division	7-1-1959	1-1-1968
	48th Infantry Brigade	9-1-1992	
	35th Infantry Division		
2-118	48th Armored Division	7-1-1959	1-1-1968
3-118	48th Armored Division	7-1-1959	1-1-1968

119th Field Artillery Regiment-National Guard

1-119	46th Infantry Division	3-15-1959	1-2-1968
	38th Infantry Division	1-2-1968	9-16-2004
	42nd Infantry Division	9-16-2004	
2-119	46th Infantry Division	3-15-1959	1-2-1968
3-119	46th Infantry Division	3-15-1959	3-15-1963

120th Field Artillery Regiment-National Guard

1-120	32nd Infantry Division	2-15-1959	12-30-1967
	32nd Infantry Brigade	12-30-1967	9-1-1997
	34th Infantry Division	9-1-1997	9-1-2001
	32nd Infantry Brigade	2-1-2001	
	34th Infantry Division		
2-120	32nd Infantry Division		

121st Field Artillery Regiment-National Guard

1-121	32nd Infantry Division	2-15-1959	12-30-1967
	257th Artillery Group	12-30-1967	---------------
	57th Field Artillery Brigade	---------------	
2-121	32nd Infantry Division	2-15-1959	4-1-1963
3-121	32nd Infantry Division	2-15-1959	12-30-1967

88

122nd Field Artillery-National Guard

1-122	33rd Infantry Division	3-1-1959	2-1-1968
2-122	33rd Infantry Division	3-1-1959	2-1-1968
	33rd Infantry Brigade	2-1-1968	9-1-1995
	Chicago Illinois	9-1-1995	9-1-1996
	34th Infantry Division	9-1-1996	9-1-1997
	35th Infantry Division	9-1-1997	Present
3-122	33rd Infantry Division	3-1-1959	2-1-1968
4-122	33rd Infantry Division	3-1-1959	4-1-1963

123rd Field Artillery Regiment-National Guard

1-123	33rd Infantry Division	3-1-1959	2-1-1968
2-123	33rd Infantry Division	3-1-1959	2-1-1968
	47th Infantry Division	2-1-1968	2-10-1991
	34th Infantry Division	2-10-1991	9-1-1996
	115th Field Artillery Brigade	9-1-1996	
3-123	Marion Illinois	9-1-1995	

124th Field Artillery Regiment-National Guard

1-124	43rd Infantry Division	3-1-1959	4-1-1963
	86th Infantry Brigade	4-1-1963	2-1-1964

125th Field Artillery Regiment-National Guard

1-125	47th Infantry Division	2-22-1959	4-1-1963
	Minnesota	4-1-1963	2-10-1991
	34th Infantry Division	2-10-1991	Present
2-125	47th Infantry Division	2-22-1959	11-1-1974
3-125	47th Infantry Division	2-22-1959	2-1-1968

126th Field Artillery Regiment-National Guard

1-126	Milwaukee Wisconsin	2-15-1959	11-5-1963
	32nd Infantry Division	2-14-1964	12-30-1967
	257th Artillery Group	12-30-1967	----------------
	57th Field Artillery Brigade	----------------	
B-1-126	Milwaukee Wisconsin	11-5-1963	2-14-1964
2-126	32nd Infantry Division	2-14-1963	12-30-1967
B-2-126	Muskego Wisconsin	12-30-1967	7-1-1971

127th Field Artillery Regiment-National Guard

1-127	35th Infantry Division	5-1-1959	4-1-1963
	127th Artillery Group	4-1-1963	12-15-1967
	130th Artillery Group	12-15-1967	---------------
	130th Field Artillery Brigade	---------------	10-1-1985
	35th Infantry Division	10-1-1985	3-1-1996
	130th Field Artillery Brigade	3-1-1996	

128th Field Artillery Regiment-National Guard

1-128	35th Infantry Division	4-15-1959	4-1-1963
	135th Artillery Group	4-1-1963	------------
	135th Field Artillery Brigade	------------	
2-128	35th Infantry Division	4-15-1959	4-1-1963
	135th Artillery Group	4-1-1963	1-15-1968
3-128	Lonejack Missouri (ADA)	5-22-1962	1-15-1968
F-128	Warrensburg Missouri	12-1-1964	1-15-1968

129th Field Artillery Regiment-National Guard

1-129	35th Infantry Division	4-15-1959	4-1-1963
	135th Artillery Group	4-1-1963	------------
	135th Field Artillery Brigade	------------	

130th Field Artillery Regiment-National Guard

1-130	130th Artillery Group	5-1-1959	12-15-1967
2-130	35th Infantry Division	5-1-1959	4-1-1963
	Kansas	4-1-1963	2-14-1964
	69th Infantry Brigade	2-14-1964	10-1-1985
	35th Infantry Division	10-1-1985	3-1-1996
	130th Field Artillery Brigade	3-1-1996	

131st Field Artillery Regiment-National Guard

1-131	36th Infantry Division	3-16-1959	1-15-1968
2-131	49th Armored Division	3-16-1959	1-15-1968
	72nd Infantry Brigade	1-15-1968	11-1-1973
	49th Armored Division	11-1-1973	1-1-1992

	49th Armored Division	9-1-1999	5-1-2004
	36th Infantry Division	5-1-2004	
3-131	49th Armored Division	3-1-1963	1-15-1968

132nd Field Artillery Regiment-National Guard

1-132	49th Armored Division	3-16-1959	1-15-1968
A-132	49th Armored Division	9-1-1994	9-1-1997
2-132	49th Armored Division	3-16-1959	1-15-1968
3-132	49th Armored Division	3-16-1959	1-15-1968
	49th Armored Division	9-1-1988	9-1-1997
4-132	Denton Texas (ADA)	8-8-1962	1-15-1968
D-132	49th Armored Division	9-1-1997	9-1-1999

133rd Field Artillery Regiment-National Guard

1-133	36th Infantry Division	3-16-1959	3-1-1963
	71st Airborne Brigade	1-15-1968	11-1-1973
	49th Armored Division	11-1-1973	9-1-1988
	50th Armored Division	9-1-1988	1-1-1992
	49th Armored Division	1-1-1992	5-1-2004
	36th Infantry Division	5-1-2004	Present
2-133	36th Infantry Division	3-16-1959	1-15-1968
3-133	36th Infantry Division	3-16-1959	1-15-1968
	Texas	1-15-1968	11-1-1973
	49th Armored Division	11-1-1973	5-1-2004
	36th Infantry Division	5-1-2004	Present
4-133	36th Infantry Division	3-16-1959	11-1-1965
	36th Infantry Brigade	11-1-1965	11-1-1973
	49th Armored Division	11-1-1973	5-1-2004
	36th Infantry Division	5-1-2004	
5-133	49th Armored Division	3-16-1959	1-15-1968
E-133	49th Armored Division	10-1-1977	9-1-1999

134th Field Artillery Regiment-National Guard

1-134	37th Infantry Division	9-1-1959	2-1-1968
	28th Infantry Division	9-1-1993	9-1-1994
	37th Infantry Division	9-1-1994	Present
2-134	37th Infantry Division	9-1-1959	2-1-1968

F-134	38th Infantry Division	9-1-1995	Present

135th Field Artillery Regiment-National Guard

1-135	37th Infantry Division	9-1-1959	2-1-1968
2-135	37th Infantry Division	9-1-19590	4-1-1963

136th Field Artillery Regiment-National Guard

1-136	37th Infantry Division	9-1-1959	2-1-1968
	38th Infantry Division	2-1-1968	3-1-1977
	73rd Infantry Brigade	3-1-1977	9-1-1992
	37th Infantry Brigade	9-1-1992	9-1-1993
2-136	37th Infantry Division	9-1-1959	2-1-1968

137th Air Defense Artillery Regiment-National Guard

1-137	137th Artillery Group (AD)	9-1-1959	4-1-1963
	371st Artillery Group (AD)	4-1-1963	2-1-1972
2-137	371st Artillery Group (AD)	9-1-1959	2-1-1968
3-137	371st Artillery Group (AD)	9-1-1959	2-1-1968

138th Air Defense Artillery Regiment-National Guard

1-138	38th Infantry Division	9-1-1988	9-1-1997
	38th Infantry Division	9-1-2000	
E-138	76th Infantry Brigade	10-1-1999	

138th Field Artillery Regiment-National Guard

1-138	138th Artillery Group	10-1-1959	5-1-1968
A-138	138th Artillery Group	10-1-1959	5-1-1974
2-138	138th Artillery Group	10-1-1959	5-13-1968
	Fort Hood Texas	5-13-1968	10-30-1968
	24th Corps Artillery	10-30-1968	10-21-1969
	138th Artillery Group	10-21-1969	----------------
	138th Field Artillery Brigade	----------------	11-1-1980
	149th Armored Brigade	11-1-1980	11-1-1985
	35th Infantry Division	11-1-1985	
	138th Fires Brigade		
3-138	138th Artillery Group	10-1-1959	5-1-1968

92

4-138	138th Artillery Group	10-1-1959	5-1-1969
5-138	138th Artillery Group	10-1-1959	5-1-1974
F-138	138th Artillery Group	3-1-1966	5-1-1968

139th Field Artillery Regiment-National Guard

1-139	38th Infantry Division	2-1-1959	12-1-1967
2-139	38th Infantry Division	2-1-1959	12-1-1967
3-139	38th Infantry Division	2-1-1959	Present
F-139	38th Infantry Division	10-1-1977	Present

140th Field Artillery Regiment-National Guard

1-140	145th Artillery Group	7-1-1959	12-1-1967
	11th Corps Artillery	12-1-1967	--------------
	1st Corps Artillery	--------------	
D-140	11th Corps Artillery	12-1-1967	
F-140	11th Corps Artillery	12-1-1964	12-1-1967

141st Field Artillery Regiment-National Guard

1-141	39th Infantry Division	7-1-1959	12-1-1967
	39th Infantry Brigade	12-1-1967	
	36th Infantry Division		
2-141	39th Infantry Division	7-1-1959	12-1-1967
3-141	39th Infantry Division	7-1-1959	5-1-1963
4-141	New Orleans Louisiana (ADA)	7-1-1959	12-1-1967
5D-141	Louisiana (ADA)	7-1-1959	5-1-1963

142nd Field Artillery Regiment-National Guard

1-142	142nd Artillery Group	5-1-1959	--------------
	142nd Field Artillery Brigade	-------------	
	142nd Fires Brigade		
2-142	142nd Artillery Group	5-1-1959	--------------
	142nd Field Artillery Brigade	-------------	
	142nd Fires Brigade		
3-142	142nd Artillery Group	5-1-1959	5-1-1963
	39th Infantry Division	5-1-1963	12-1-1967
4-142	142nd Artillery Group	5-1-1959	12-1-1967

5-142	142nd Artillery Group	5-1-1959	12-1-1967
F-142	142nd Fires Brigade		

143rd Field Artillery Regiment-National Guard

1-143	49th Infantry Division	5-1-1959	1-29-1968
	143rd Artillery Group	1-29-1968	11-1-1971
	California	11-1-1971	1-13-1974
	40th Infantry Division	1-13-1974	
2-143	49th Infantry Division	5-1-1959	1-29-1968
3-143	49th Infantry Division	5-1-1959	12-4-1965
	49th Infantry Brigade	12-4-1965	1-13-1974
4-143	49th Infantry Division	5-1-1959	1-29-1968
5-143	49th Infantry Division	5-1-1959	1-29-1968
6-143	49th Infantry Division	5-1-1959	3-1-1963

144th Field Artillery Regiment-National Guard

1-144	40th Armored Division	7-1-1959	1-29-1968
	40th Armored Brigade	1-29-1968	1-13-1974
	40th Infantry Division	1-13-1974	12-1-1993
	40th Infantry Division	10-1-1997	Present
2-144	40th Armored Division	7-1-1959	1-29-1968
	143rd Artillery Group	1-29-1968	11-1-1971
	California	11-1-1971	1-13-1974
	40th Infantry Division	1-13-1974	10-1-1997
3-144	40th Armored Division	7-1-1959	1-29-1968
	40th Infantry Brigade	1-29-1968	1-13-1974
	40th Infantry Division	1-13-1974	10-1-1997
4-144	40th Armored Division	7-1-1959	1-29-1968
D-144	40th Infantry Division	12-1-1993	
5-144	40th Armored Division	3-1-1963	1-29-1968
F-144	40th Infantry Division	12-1-1976	

145th Field Artillery Regiment-National Guard

1-145	11th Corps Artillery	7-1-1959	--------------
	1st Corps Artillery	-------------	
	65th Fires Brigade		
2-145	11th Corps Artillery	7-1-1959	12-1-1967

146th Field Artillery Regiment-National Guard

1-146	41st Infantry Division	4-15-1959	1-1-1968
2-146	41st Infantry Division	4-15-1959	1-1-1968
	81st Infantry Brigade	1-1-1968	8-1-2000
	81st Armored Brigade	8-1-2000	
	40th Infantry Division		

147th Field Artillery Regiment-National Guard

1-147	147th Artillery Group	10-21-1959	-------------
	147th Field Artillery Brigade	----------------	
2-147	147th Artillery Group	10-21-1959	-------------
	147th Field Artillery Brigade	----------------	
3-147	147th Artillery Group	10-21-1959	1-4-1968
4-147	147th Artillery Group	10-21-1959	1-4-1968

148th Field Artillery Regiment-National Guard

1-148	Lewiston Idaho	7-1-1959	12-11-1967
	116th Cavalry Brigade	9-1-1989	
	34th Infantry Division		

150th Field Artillery Regiment-National Guard

1-150	38th Infantry Division	2-1-1959	8-1-1975
2-150	38th Infantry Division	2-1-1959	9-1-1996
	Bloomington Indiana	9-1-1996	

151st Field Artillery Regiment-National Guard

1-151	47th Infantry Division	2-22-1959	2-10-1991
	34th Infantry Division	2-10-1991	9-1-1996
	135th Field Artillery Brigade	9-1-1996	
2-151	47th Infantry Division	2-22-1959	4-1-1963
3-151	47th Infantry Division	2-22-1959	2-1-1968
E-151	47th Infantry Division	10-1-1977	2-10-1991
	34th Infantry Division	2-10-1991	
F-151	34th Infantry Division	9-1-1995	

152nd Field Artillery Regiment-National Guard

1-152	Caribou Maine	5-1-1959	
F-152	Gardiner Maine	12-1-1964	12-31-1967

156th Field Artillery Regiment-National Guard

1-156	187th Artillery Group	3-16-1959	4-15-1963
	27th Armored Division	4-15-1963	2-1-1968
	50th Armored Division	2-1-1968	4-1-1975
	27th Infantry Brigade	4-1-1986	9-1-2004
2-156	27th Armored Division	4-15-1963	2-1-1968

157th Field Artillery Regiment-National Guard

1-157	169th Artillery Group	2-1-1959	-------------
	169th Field Artillery Brigade	------------	
	169th Fires Brigade		
2-157	169th Artillery Group	2-1-1959	-------------
	169th Field Artillery Brigade	------------	
	169th Fires Brigade		
3-157	169th Artillery Group	2-1-1959	2-1-1968
4-157	169th Artillery Group	2-1-1959	2-1-1968

158th Field Artillery Regiment-National Guard

1-158	45th Infantry Division	5-1-1959	1-2-1968
	145th Artillery Group	1-2-1968	------------
	45th Field Artillery Brigade	------------	
	45th Fires Brigade		
2-158	45th Infantry Division	5-1-1959	4-1-1963
	Oklahoma	8-1-1975	

160th Field Artillery Regiment-National Guard

1-160	45th Infantry Division	5-1-1959	1-2-1968
	45th Infantry Brigade	1-2-1968	
	35th Infantry Division		
2-160	45th Infantry Division	5-1-1959	4-1-1963

161st Field Artillery Regiment-National Guard

1-161	130th Artillery Group	5-1-1959	4-1-1963
	69th Infantry Brigade	4-1-1963	2-14-1964
	130th Artillery Group	2-14-1964	--------------
	130th Field Artillery Brigade	--------------	11-1-1985
	35th Infantry Division	11-1-1985	
E-161	35th Infantry Division	9-1-1988	
F-161	35th Infantry Division	10-1-1996	

162nd Field Artillery Regiment-National Guard

1-162	Hato Rey Puerto Rico	2-1-1959	5-1-1964
	92nd Infantry Brigade	5-1-1964	12-31-1967
	Hato Rey Puerto Rico	12-31-1967	
2-162	Hato Rey Puerto Rico	2-15-1959	12-31-1967
	92nd Infantry Brigade	12-31-1967	
	29th Infantry Division		
3-162	San Juan Puerto Rico (ADA)	2-15-1959	5-1-1963
	Hato Rey Puerto Rico FA	10-1-1997	

163rd Field Artillery Regiment-National Guard

1-163	38th Infantry Division	3-1-1977	9-1-1994
	76th Infantry Brigade	9-1-1994	
	38th Infantry Division		

166th Field Artillery Regiment-National Guard

1-166	28th Infantry Division FA	6-1-1959	2-17-1968
	28th Infantry Division	4-1-1975	10-1-1975
2-166	218th Artillery Group (AD) ADA	6-1-1959	4-1-1963
	213th Artillery Group (AD)	4-1-1963	2-17-1968
	Worchester Pennsylvania	2-17-1968	9-30-1974
3-166	213th Artillery Group (AD) ADA	6-1-1959	4-1-1963
4-166	213th Artillery Group (AD) ADA	6-1-1959	2-17-1968

168th Field Artillery Regiment-National Guard

1-168	34th Infantry Division	5-1-1959	4-1-1963
	168th Artillery Group	4-1-1963	2-1-1968
	67th Infantry Brigade	2-1-1968	11-1-1985
	35th Infantry Division	11-1-1985	9-1-1996
2-168	34th Infantry Division	5-1-1959	4-1-1963
	168th Artillery Group	4-1-1963	2-1-1964
	67th Infantry Brigade	2-1-1964	2-1-1968

170th Field Artillery Regiment-National Guard

1-170	187th Artillery Group	3-16-1959	4-15-1963
	27th Armored Division	4-15-1963	2-1-1968

171st Field Artillery Regiment-National Guard

1-171	45th Infantry Division	4-1-1963	1-2-1968
	145th Artillery Group	1-2-1968	------------
	45th Field Artillery Brigade	------------	
	45th Fires Brigade		

172nd Field Artillery Regiment-National Guard

1-172	2nd Corps Artillery	4-1-1963	12-1-1967
	197th Artillery Group	12-1-1967	--------------
	197th Field Artillery Brigade	--------------	
	197th Fires Brigade		
2-172	2nd Corps Artillery	4-1-1963	12-1-1967

174th Air Defense Artillery Regiment-National Guard

1-174	191st Artillery Group (AD)	9-1-1959	4-1-1963
	371st Artillery Group (AD)	4-1-1963	2-1-1968
	Cincinnati Ohio		
2-174	371st Artillery Group (AD)	9-1-1959	2-1-1972
	McConnelsville Ohio	2-1-1972	8-1-1975
	38th Infantry Division	8-1-1975	10-1-1989
	McConnelsville Ohio	10-1-1989	
3D-174	371st Artillery Group (AD)	9-1-1959	2-1-1968

175th Field Artillery Regiment-National Guard

1-175	Olivia Minnesota	2-22-1959	4-1-1963
	47th Infantry Division	4-1-1963	2-10-1991
	34th Infantry Division	2-10-1991	9-1-1992

176th Air Defense Artillery Regiment-National Guard

1-176	218th Artillery Group (AD)	6-1-1959	4-1-1963
2-176	218th Artillery Group (AD)	6-1-1959	4-1-1963
	213th Artillery Group (AD)	4-1-1963	2-17-1968
	Pennsylvania	2-17-1968	9-30-1974

177th Air Defense Artillery Regiment-National Guard

1-177	210th Artillery Group (AD)	3-15-1959	3-15-1963
	Detroit Michigan	3-15-1963	9-30-1974
2-177	210th Artillery Group (AD)	3-15-1959	3-15-1963

178th Field Artillery Regiment-National Guard

1-178	51st Infantry Division	4-1-1959	4-1-1963
	151st Artillery Group	4-1-1963	1-1-1968
	30th Infantry Division	1-1-1968	11-30-1973
	218th Infantry Brigade	11-30-1973	
	35th Infantry Division		
2-178	51st Infantry Division	4-1-1959	1-1-1968
3-178	51st Infantry Division	4-1-1959	4-1-1963
	151st Artillery Group	4-1-1963	------------
	151st Field Artillery Brigade	------------	
4-178	51st Infantry Division	4-1-1959	4-1-1963
	151st Artillery Group	4-1-1963	------------
	151st Field Artillery Brigade	------------	9-1-1993

179th Field Artillery Regiment-National Guard

| 1-179 | 48th Armored Division | 7-1-1959 | 1-1-1968 |

179th Air Defense Artillery Regiment-National Guard

E-179	48th Infantry Brigade	10-1-1999	

180th Field Artillery Regiment-National Guard

1-180	Mesa Arizona	3-1-1959	4-1-1976
	153rd Artillery Group	4-1-1976	------------
	153rd Field Artillery Brigade	------------	9-1-1997
	11th Armored Cavalry Regiment	9-1-1997	Present
2-180	153rd Artillery Group	4-1-1976	------------
	153rd Field Artillery Brigade	------------	9-1-1992
	40th Infantry Division	9-1-1997	10-1-1999
	153rd Field Artillery Brigade	10-1-1999	
	40th Infantry Division		

181st Field Artillery Regiment-National Guard

1-181	30th Armored Division	3-1-1959	11-1-1973
	196th Artillery Group	11-1-1973	--------------
	196th Field Artillery Brigade	--------------	
2-181	30th Armored Division	4-1-1963	2-1-1968

182nd Field Artillery regiment-National Guard

1-182	46th Infantry Division	3-15-1959	1-2-1968
	157th Artillery Group	1-2-1968	9-30-1974
	Detroit Michigan	9-30-1974	
2-182	46th Infantry Division	3-15-1959	1-2-1968
	157th Artillery Group	1-2-1968	9-30-1974
3-182	46th Infantry Division	3-15-1959	1-2-1968

184th Air Defense Artillery Regiment-National Guard

1-184	202nd Artillery Group (AD)	3-1-1959	4-1-1963

185th Field Artillery Regiment-National Guard

1-185	34th Infantry Division	5-1-1959	3-1-1963
	34th Artillery Group	3-1-1963	1-1-1968
	Davenport Iowa	1-1-1968	9-30-1974

2-185	34th Infantry Division	5-1-1959	3-1-1963
3-185	34th Infantry Division	5-1-1959	3-1-1963
4-185	34th Infantry Division	5-1-1959	3-1-1963
	34th Artillery Group	3-1-1963	1-1-1968

186th Field Artillery Regiment-National Guard

1-186	27th Armored Division	3-16-1959	4-15-1963
	187th Artillery Group	4-15-1963	2-1-1968

187th Field Artillery Regiment-National Guard

1-187	187th Artillery Group	3-16-1959	2-1-1968
	209th Artillery Group	2-1-1968	4-1-1975
	42nd Infantry Division	4-1-1975	9-1-1991
2-187	Brooklyn New York	5-1-1962	4-15-1963
	187th Artillery Group	4-15-1963	2-1-1968

188th Air Defense Artillery Regiment-National Guard

1-188	6th Infantry Division	10-1-1988	7-6-1994
	Grand Forks North Dakota	7-6-1994	9-1-1995
	40th Infantry Division	9-1-1995	
E-188	41st Infantry Brigade	10-1-1999	
F-188	116th Cavalry Brigade	10-1-1999	

189th Field Artillery Regiment-National Guard

1-189	45th Infantry Division	5-1-1959	1-2-1968
	145th Artillery Group	1-2-1968	------------
	45th Field Artillery Brigade	------------	9-1-1996
2-189	45th Infantry Division	5-1-1959	1-2-1968

190th Field Artillery Regiment-National Guard

1-190	154th Artillery Group	5-1-1959	4-1-1963
	115th Field Artillery Brigade	10-1-1995	
2-190	154th Artillery Group	5-1-1959	4-1-1963
	Montana	4-1-1963	2-1-1968

192nd Field Artillery Regiment-National Guard

1-192	Cromwell Connecticut	5-1-1963	12-16-1967
2-192	Stamford Connecticut	5-1-1963	12-16-1967
	26th Infantry Division	12-16-1967	9-1-1993
	43rd Field Artillery Brigade	9-1-1993	4-1-1997
	29th Infantry Division	4-1-1997	9-1-2003
F-192	Hartford Connecticut	12-1-1964	12-16-1967

194th Field Artillery Regiment-National Guard

1-194	Humboldt Iowa	3-1-1959	4-1-1963
	34th Artillery Group	4-1-1963	1-1-1968
	47th Infantry Division	1-1-1968	2-10-1991
	34th Infantry Division	2-10-1991	Present

197th Field Artillery Regiment-National Guard

1-197	197th Artillery Group	2-1-1959	12-1-1967
A-197	197th Artillery Group	12-1-1967	9-1-1978
	50th Armored Division	9-1-1978	9-1-1993
2-197	197th Artillery Group	2-1-1959	------------
	197th Field Artillery Brigade	------------	
	197th Fires Brigade		
3-197	197th Artillery Group	2-1-1959	5-13-1968
	Fort Bragg North Carolina	5-13-1968	9-20-1968
	23rd Artillery Group	9-20-1968	9-3-1969
	197th Artillery Group	9-3-1969	------------
	197th Field Artillery Brigade	------------	9-1-1992
4-197	197th Artillery Group	2-1-1959	2-1-1963

198th Air Defense Artillery Regiment-National Guard

1-198	261st Artillery Brigade (AD)	5-1-1959	1-1-1970
2-198	261st Artillery Brigade (AD)	5-1-1959	1-1-1970
3-198	261st Artillery Brigade (AD)	5-1-1959	1-1-1970
4-198	261st Artillery Brigade (AD)	5-1-1959	1-31-1968
5-198	261st Artillery Brigade (AD)	5-1-1959	4-1-1963
6-198	261st Artillery Brigade (AD)	5-1-1959	1-31-1968

200th Air Defense Artillery Regiment-National Guard

1-200	111th ADA Brigade	9-1-1959	9-1-1975
	49th Armored Division	9-1-1975	9-1-1993
	111th ADA Brigade	9-1-1993	
2-200	111th ADA Brigade	9-1-1959	9-1-1975
	47th Infantry Division	9-1-1975	11-14-1988
	111th ADA Brigade	11-14-1988	9-1-1995
	111th ADA Brigade	12-1-1997	
3-200	111th ADA Brigade	9-1-1959	9-1-1975
	50th Armored Division	9-1-1975	9-1-1993
	111th ADA Brigade	9-1-1993	
4-200	111th ADA Brigade	9-1-1959	9-1-1975
	40th Infantry Division	9-1-1975	10-1-1988
	111th ADA Brigade	10-1-1988	
5-200	111th ADA Brigade	9-1-1959	12-15-1967
	111th ADA Brigade	7-1-1987	9-30-1988
6-200	111th ADA Brigade	9-1-1959	12-15-1967
	Santa Fe New Mexico	9-1-1989	9-1-1996
	42nd Infantry Division	9-1-1996	10-1-1998
7-200	111th ADA Brigade	3-1-1987	12-1-1997
7D-200	111th ADA Brigade	9-1-1959	12-15-1967
8D-200	111th ADA Brigade	9-1-1959	12-15-1967

201st Air Defense Artillery Regiment-National Guard

E-201	92nd Infantry Brigade

201st Field Artillery Regiment-National Guard

1-201	Fairmont West Virginia	3-1-1959

202nd Air Defense Artillery Regiment-National Guard

1-202	202nd Artillery Group (AD)	3-1-1959	10-8-1963
	Arlington Heights Illinois	10-8-1963	9-30-1974
	47th Infantry Division	11-14-1988	2-10-1991
	34th Infantry Division	2-10-1991	
	42nd Infantry Division		

2-202	202nd Artillery Group (AD)	3-1-1959	10-8-1963
	35th Infantry Division	10-26-1994	
E-202	45th Infantry Brigade	10-1-1999	
F-202	39th Infantry Brigade	10-1-1999	
G-202	30th Infantry Brigade	10-1-1999	9-1-2002
	30th Armored Brigade	9-1-2002	
H-202	256th Infantry Brigade	10-1-1999	

202nd Field Artillery Regiment-National Guard

1-202	Las Cruces New Mexico	9-1-1995	

203rd Air Defense Artillery Regiment-National Guard

1-203	31st Infantry Division	5-2-1959	4-15-1963
	Huntsville Alabama	9 1 1995	
2-203	Alabama	5-2-1959	1-15-1968
3-203	226th Artillery Group (AD)	5-2-1959	1-15-1968
	Alabama	1-15-1968	12-1-1969
4-203	226th Artillery Group (AD)	5-2-1959	4-15-1963
E-203	31st Armored Brigade		

204th Air Defense Artillery Regiment-National Guard

1-204	Newton Mississippi	10-1-1994	
E-204	155th Armored Brigade	10-1-1999	

205th Field Artillery Regiment-National Guard

1-205	115th Artillery Brigade (AD)	4-15-1959	3-1-1963
	205th Artillery Group	3-1-1963	1-1-1968
2-205	115th Artillery Brigade (AD)	4-15-1959	3-1-1963
	Redmond Washington	3-1-1963	1-1-1968
3-205	115th Artillery Brigade (AD)	4-15-1959	3-1-1963
4-205	115th Artillery Brigade (AD)	4-15-1959	3-1-1963
5D-205	115th Artillery Brigade (AD)	4-15-1959	3-1-1963

206th Field Artillery Regiment-National Guard

1-206	39th Infantry Division	6-1-1959	5-1-1963
	39th Infantry Brigade	9-1-1996	
	36th Infantry Division		

2-206	39th Infantry Division	6-1-1959	12-1-1967
3-206	39th Infantry Division	6-1-1959	12-1-1967
5-206	39th Infantry Brigade	12-1-1967	9-1-1996

209th Field Artillery Regiment-National Guard

1-209	209th Artillery Group (AD)	3-16-1959	4-15-1963
	209th Artillery Group	4-15-1963	--------------
	209th Field Artillery Brigade	--------------	9-1-1989
	42nd Infantry Division	9-1-1989	9-1-1991
2-209	Lancaster New York	4-15-1963	4-1-1970
3D-209	209th Artillery Group (AD)	3-16-1959	4-15-1963

210th Air Defense Artillery Regiment-National Guard

1-210	209th Artillery Group (AD)	3-16-1959	10-1-1960

211th Field Artillery Regiment-National Guard

1-211	102nd Artillery Group	5-1-1959	12-19-1967
	North Bedford Massachusetts	12-19-1967	5-13-1968
	Fort Benning Georgia	5-13-1968	9-3-1969
	North Bedford Massachusetts	9-3-1969	4-1-1975
	26th Infantry Division	4-1-1975	9-1-1993
2-211	102nd Artillery Group	5-1-1959	3-1-1963
3-211	102nd Artillery Group	5-1-1959	12-19-1967
4-211	102nd Artillery Group	5-1-1959	12-19-1967
5D-211	102nd Artillery Group	5-1-1959	10-31-1961
E-211	26th Infantry Division	9-1-1988	9-1-1993

212th Air Defense Artillery Regiment-National Guard

1-212	244th Artillery Group (AD)	3-16-1959	4-15-1963

213th Air Defense Artillery Regiment-National Guard

1-213	213th Artillery Group (AD)	6-1-1959	4-1-1963
	28th Infantry Division	10-1-1990	
2-213	213th Artillery Group (AD)	6-1-1959	4-1-1963
3-213	213th Artillery Group (AD)	6-1-1959	4-1-1963

4-213	Reading Pennsylvania	6-1-1959	2-17-1968
5D-213	213th Artillery Group (AD)	6-1-1959	4-1-1963

214th Field Artillery Regiment-National Guard

1-214	108th Artillery Brigade (AD)	7-1-1959	4-16-1963
	48th Armored Division	4-16-1963	1-1-1968
	118th Artillery Group	1-1-1968	------------
	118th Field Artillery Brigade	------------	11-10-1992
	Elberton Georgia	11-10-1992	
2-214	108th Artillery Brigade (AD)	7-1-1959	5-1-1962
	118th Artillery Group	1-1-1968	------------
	118th Field Artillery Brigade	------------	11-10-1992
3-214	108th Artillery Brigade (AD)	7-1-1959	4-16-1963
4-214	108th Artillery Brigade (AD)	7-1-1959	5-1-1962
5D-214	108th Artillery Brigade (AD)	7 1-1959	4-16-1963

216th Air Defense Artillery Regiment-National Guard

1-216	34th Infantry Division	9-1-1997
D-216	29th Infantry Brigade	10-1-1999
E-216	81st Infantry Brigade	10-1-1999

218th Field Artillery Regiment-National Guard

1-218	41st Infantry Division	4-1-1959	3-1-1968
2-218	41st Infantry Division	4-1-1959	11-1-1965
	41st Infantry Brigade	11-1-1965	
	40th Infantry Division		
3-218	41st Infantry Division	4-1-1959	3-1-1968

221st Air Defense Artillery Regiment-National Guard

1-221	121st Artillery Group (AD)	4-1-1959	11-1-1965
	Nevada	11-1-1965	12-15-1967
2-221	121st Artillery Group (AD)	4-1-1959	11-1-1965
3D-221	121st Artillery Group (AD)	4-1-1959	5-1-1962

222nd Field Artillery Regiment-National Guard

1-222	11th Corps Artillery	7-1-1959	12-1-1967
2-222	11th Corps Artillery	7-1-1959	------------
	1st Corps Artillery	------------	
	65th Fires Brigade		

229th Field Artillery Regiment-National Guard

1-229	28th Infantry Division	6-1-1959	10-1-1995
	28th Infantry Division		
D-229	28th Infantry Division	10-1-1995	

230th Field Artillery Regiment-National Guard

| 1-230 | 30th Infantry Division | 1-1-1968 | 11-30-1973 |
| | 48th Infantry Brigade | 11-30-1973 | 11-10-1992 |

233rd Air Defense Artillery Regiment-National Guard

| 1-233 | Booneville Arkansas | 10-1-1989 | 10-1-1996 |

235th Field Artillery Regiment-National Guard

| 1-235 | 35th Infantry Division | 5-1-1959 | 4-1-1963 |

240th Air Defense Artillery Regiment-National Guard

| 1-240 | Bangor Maine | 5-15-1959 | 6-1-1961 |

241st Field Artillery Regiment-National Guard

1-241	211th Artillery Group (AD)	5-1-1959	3-1-1963
	Natick Massachusetts (ADA)	3-1-1963	11-1-1974
	26th Infantry Division (FA)	11-1-1974	12-1-1975
2-241	211th Artillery Group (AD)	5-1-1959	3-1-1963
	211th Artillery Group (AD)	5-1-1959	5-1-1962

242nd Air Defense Artillery Regiment-National Guard

1-242	208th Artillery Group (AD)	5-1-1959	5-1-1963
2-242	43rd Infantry Division	5-1-1959	5-1-1963
3-242	208th Artillery Group (AD)	5-1-1959	5-1-1963
4D-242	208th Artillery Group (AD)	5-1-1959	5-1-1963

243rd Air Defense Artillery Regiment-National Guard

1-243	Providence Rhode Island	4-1-1959	5-1-1962
2-243	Coventry Rhode Island	4-1-1959	3-18-1963
B-2-243	Coventry Rhode Island	4-1-1959	- -1971

244th Air Defense Artillery Regiment-National Guard

1-244	244th Artillery Group (AD)	3-16-1959	4-15-1963
	Roslyn New York	4-15-1963	9-30-1974
2-244	187th Artillery Group	4-15-1963	2-1-1968

245th Air Defense Artillery Regiment-National Guard

1-245	244th Artillery Group (AD)	3-16-1959	4-15-1963

246th Field Artillery Regiment-National Guard

1-246	29th Infantry Division	3-1-1959	2-1-1968
	224th Artillery Group	2-1-1968	12-1-1971
	28th Infantry Division	12-1-1971	6-1-1975
	116th Infantry Brigade	6-1-1975	6-1-1986
	29th Infantry Division	6-1-1986	
2-246	29th Infantry Division	3-1-1959	2-1-1968
3-246	107th Artillery Brigade (AD)	3-1-1959	2-1-1968
4D-246	107th Artillery Brigade (AD)	3-1-1959	3-22-1963

248th Field Artillery Regiment-National Guard

1-248	41st Infantry Division	4-1-1959	3-1-1963
	205th Artillery Group	3-1-1963	3-1-1968

249th Air Defense Artillery Regiment-National Guard

1-249	249th Artillery Group (AD)	4-1-1959	4-1-1963
2-249	249th Artillery Group (AD)	4-1-1959	3-1-1968
3-249	249th Artillery Group (AD)	4-1-1959	6-17-1971
4D-249	249th Artillery Group (AD)	4-1-1959	3-1-1968

250th Air Defense Artillery Regiment-National Guard

1-250	233rd Artillery Group (AD)	7-1-1959	5-1-1962
	San Francisco California	5-1-1962	9-30-1974
2-250	233rd Artillery Group (AD)	7-1-1959	5-1-1962
3-250	233rd Artillery Group (AD)	7-1-1959	5-1-1962

251st Air Defense Artillery Regiment-National Guard

1-251	234th Artillery Group (AD)	7-1-1959	5-1-1962
2-251	234th Artillery Group (AD)	7-1-1959	5-1-1962
3-251	234th Artillery Group (AD)	7-1-1959	5-1-1962
4-251	234th Artillery Group (AD)	7-1-1959	5-1-1962
	San Pedro California	5-1-1962	9-30-1974

252nd Air Defense Artillery Regiment-National Guard

1-252	30th Infantry Division (FA)	4-1-1959	3-10-1963
2-252	252nd Artillery Group (AD)	4-1-1959	3-10-1963
3-252	252nd Artillery Group (AD)	4-1-1959	3-10-1963

254th Air Defense Artillery Regiment-National Guard

1-254	254th Artillery Group (AD)	3-1-1959	1-25-1963
	Livingston New Jersey	1-25-1963	2-1-1968
2-254	254th Artillery Group (AD)	3-1-1959	1-25-1963

258th Field Artillery Regiment-National Guard

1-258	42nd Infantry Division	3-16-1959	Present
2-258	42nd Infantry Division	3-16-1959	2-1-1968
3-258	42nd Infantry Division	3-16-1959	4-15-1963
4-258	42nd Infantry Division	3-16-1959	8-1-1973
E-258	42nd Infantry Division	3-16-1959	9-1-1993

263rd Air Defense Artillery Regiment-National Guard

1-263	163rd Artillery Group (AD)	4-1-1959	1-1-1968
	263rd ADA Brigade	1-1-1968	10-1-1996
	263rd AAMDC	10-1-1996	Present

2-263	163rd Artillery Group (AD)	4-1-1959	1-1-1968
	Anderson South Carolina	1-1-1968	8-1-1975
	26th Infantry Division	8-1-1975	9-1-1993
	263rd ADA Brigade	9-1-1993	10-1-1998
	49th Armored Division	10-1-1998	
3-263	163rd Artillery Group (AD)	4-1-1959	4-1-1963
4D-263	163rd Artillery Group (AD)	4-1-1959	4-1-1963
E-263	218th Infantry Brigade	10-1-1999	

265th Air Defense Artillery Regiment-National Guard

1-265	Jacksonville Florida	4-16-1959	2-15-1963
	164th Artillery Group (AD)	2-15-1963	1-20-1968
	West Palm Beach Florida	1-20-1968	10-1-1987
	164th ADA Brigade		10-1-1998
	32nd AAMDC	10-1-1998	Present
2-265	Sarasota Florida	4-16-1959	2-15-1963
	164th Artillery Group (AD)	2-15-1963	1-20-1968
	164th ADA Brigade	1-20-1968	10-1-1998
	32nd AAMDC	10-1-1998	Present
3-265	164th ADA Brigade	10-1-1987	10-1-1998
	32nd AAMDC	10-1-1998	Present
E-265	53rd Infantry Brigade	10-1-1999	
16D-265	164th Artillery Group (AD)	2-15-1963	1-20-1968
17D-265	164th Artillery Group (AD)	2-15-1963	1-20-1968

270th Field Artillery Regiment-National Guard

1-270	27th Armored Division	3-16-1959	4-15-1963

278th Air Defense Artillery Regiment-National Guard

1-278	226th Artillery Group (AD)	5-2-1959	1-15-1968
2-278	226th Artillery Group (AD)	5-2-1959	1-15-1968
3D-278	226th Artillery Group (AD)	5-2-1959	1-15-1968

280th Air Defense Artillery Regiment-National Guard

1-280	224th Artillery Group (AD)	6-1-1959	4-1-1963
B-1-280	Vienna Virginia	4-1-1963	- -1965
2-280	224th Artillery Group (AD)	6-1-1959	4-1-1963

298th Air Defense Artillery Regiment-National Guard

1-298	298th Artillery Group (AD)	2-15-1959	12-15-1967
	Hawaii	12-15-1967	4-1-1970
2-298	298th Artillery Group (AD)	2-15-1959	12-15-1967

300th Field Artillery Regiment-National Guard

2-300	115th Field Artillery Brigade	9-1-1996	

319th Field Artillery Regiment-Active Component

A-319	82nd Airborne Division	9-1-1957	7-1-1958
1-319	82nd Airborne Division	5-24-1964	Present
B-319	82nd Airborne Division	9-1-1957	2-1-1964
2-319	101st Airborne Division	2-1-1964	7-31-1972
	82nd Airborne Division	10-2-1986	Present
C-319	82nd Airborne Division	9-1-1957	6-24-1960
	25th Infantry Division	6-24-1960	7-1-1961
	Okinawa	7-1-1961	6-25-1963
3-319	173rd Airborne Brigade	6-25-1963	1-14-1972
	101st Airborne Division	1-14-1972	10-2-1986
	82nd Airborne Division	10-2-1986	Present
D-319	101st Airborne Division	4-25-1957	4-3-1964
	Southern European Task Force	10-16-1986	6-12-2000
	173rd Airborne Brigade	6-12-2000	
4-319	173rd Airborne Brigade		
E-319	101st Airborne Division	4-25-1957	4-3-1964

320th Field Artillery Regiment-Active Component

A-320	11th Airborne Division	3-1-1957	7-1-1958
1-320	82nd Airborne Division	12-7-1962	10-2-1986
	101st Airborne Division	10-2-1986	Present
B-320	11th Airborne Division	3-1-1957	7-1-1958
2-320	101st Airborne Division	12-3-1962	Present
C-320	11th Airborne Division	3-1-1957	7-1-1958
	82nd Airborne Division	7-1-1960	5-24-1964
3-320	82nd Airborne Division	7-15-1968	12-15-1969
	101st Airborne Division	10-2-1986	Present

D-320	82nd Airborne Division	9-1-1957	5-24-1964
	193rd Infantry Brigade	10-2-1986	10-15-1994
4-320	101st Airborne Division	9-16-2004	Present
E-320	Berlin Brigade	10-2-1986	10-15-1994

321st Field Artillery Regiment-Active Component

A-321	101st Airborne Division	4-25-1957	2-3-1964
1-321	101st Airborne Division	2-3-1964	10-2-1986
	18th Field Artillery Brigade	1-16-1996	
	18th Fires Brigade		
B-321	101st Airborne Division	4-25-1957	2-3-1964
2-321	82nd Airborne Division	5-24-1964	10-2-1986
	82nd Airborne Division	6-16-2006	Present
C-321	USAFATC-Fort Sill Oklahoma (T)	2-28-1987	1-15-1996
	18th Field Artillery Brigade	1-16-1996	
	18th Fires Brigade		
D-321	11th Airborne Division	3-1-1957	7-1-1958
E-321	11th Airborne Division	3-1-1957	7-1-1958

333rd Field Artillery Regiment-Active Component

1-333	Germany	9-16-1962	6-24-1964
BA-B	Germany	3-16-1960	6-24-1964
1-333	Fort Bliss Texas	5-1-1965	1-30-1970
	Germany	7-2-1973	
A-333	1st Cavalry Division	8-16-1987	12-16-1992
2-333	Germany	2-1-1958	6-25-1964
B-333	7th Infantry Division	7-21-1978	4-2-1985
3-333	Fort Sill Oklahoma	7-25-1966	5-15-1970
	Fort Sill Oklahoma	6-24-1972	12-1-1974
C-333	8th Infantry Division	9-21-1978	1-17-1992
	1st Armored Division	1-17-1992	2-15-1997
4-333	Fort Sill Oklahoma	10-1-1957	10-15-1963
	South Bend Indiana	9-1-1971	9-1-1991
E-333	Fort Carson Colorado	2-5-1967	5-26-1967
	9th Infantry Division	11-21-1977	6-15-1991
F-333	Fort Carson Colorado	2-5-1967	5-26-1967
	3rd Armored Division	9-21-1978	11-15-1991
	210th Fires Brigade	11-30-2006	Present
G-333	Fort Carson Colorado	2-5-1967	5-26-1967
	24th Infantry Division	9-30-1978	2-16-1996

369th Field Artillery Regiment-National Guard

1-369	187th Artillery Group	3-16-1959	2-1-1968

377th Field Artillery Regiment-Active Component

A-377	101st Airborne Division	4-25-1957	5-21-1965
	101st Airborne Division	12-20-1968	6-15-1986
1-377	18th Field Artillery Brigade	1-16-1996	
	18th Fires Brigade		
B-377	82nd Airborne Division	9-1-1957	7-8-1965
	Afghanistan	- -2003	11-6-2005
2-377	Germany	4-1-1974	7-16-1987
	25th Infantry Division	11-6-2005	Present
C-377	11th Airborne Division	3-1-1957	7-1-1958
3-377	11th Air Assault Division	7-18-1963	7-1-1965

487th Field Artillery Regiment-National Guard

1-487	29th Infantry Brigade	11-1-1965	
	40th Infantry Division		

517th Air Defense Artillery Regiment-Active Component

1-517	Mudiliem Illinois	9-1-1958	12-23-1960
2-517	Carelton Michigan	9-1-1958	2-8-1963
3-517	Selfridge AFB Michigan	9-1-1958	9-13-1972
4-517	Fort Clayton Canal Zone	9-1-1958	3-31-1970
5-517	Dyess AFB Texas	9-1-1958	6-25-1966
6-517	Fort Bliss Texas	9-1-1958	---------------
	Germany	------------	9-28-1972
16D-517	Fort Bliss Texas	9-1-1958	9-28-1960

562nd Air Defense Artillery Regiment-Active Component

1-562	Fort Meade Maryland	9-1-1958	12-11-1962
2-562	Ladd AFB Alaska	9-11-1958	6-30-1971
3-562	Suitland Maryland	9-1-1958	12-15-1961
4-562	Dallas Texas	6-15-1959	----------------
	Duncanville Texas	--------------	2-10-1969

5-562	Barksdale AFB Louisiana	3-17-1960	3-25-1966
	Fort Campbell Kentucky	5-1-1972	9-13-1972
6-562	Fort Bliss Texas	5-7-1962	--------------
	Germany	------------	9-13-1972
12D-562	Fort Meade Maryland	9-1-1958	1-23-1959
16D-562	Fort Bliss Texas	9-1-1958	9-17-1962

623rd Field Artillery Regiment-National Guard

1-623	138th Artillery Group	3-1-1969	--------------
	138th Field Artillery Brigade	------------	
	138th Fires Brigade		

Armor-Cavalry Battalions 1957-2011

1st Cavalry Regiment-Active Component

1-1	1st Armored Division		2-1-1957	Present
2-1	3rd Armored Division		10-1-1957	7-1-1963
	2nd Armored Division		7-1-1963	5-21-1991
	2nd Armored Division		12-16-1992	1-16-1996
	2nd Infantry Division	RSTA		
3-1	1st Armored Division		6-16-1967	5-10-1971
	5th Infantry Division		- -1990	11-24-1992
	3rd Infantry Division	RSTA		
C-1	3rd Infantry Division			Present
4-1	United States Military Academy		5-15-1958	Present
E-1	11th Infantry Brigade		7-1-1966	2-15-1969
	23rd Infantry Division		2-15-1969	11-30-1971
	172nd Infantry Brigade		12-31-1972	4-15-1986
	172nd Infantry Brigade		4-17-1998	11-23-2003
5-1	25th Infantry Division	RSTA	12-16-2006	Present
6-1	1st Armored Division		6-19-1967	11-10-1971
	1st Armored Division	RSTA		
F-1	1st Armored Division			Present
7-1	Fort Knox Kentucky		4-25-1967	2-28-1968
	1st Aviation Brigade		2-28-1968	4-7-1972
	Fort Knox Kentucky		4-7-1972	- -1976
	3rd Infantry Division			
G-1	Fort Knox Kentucky		- -1976	- -1979
8-1	Fort Knox Kentucky		8-25-1967	4-7-1972
H-1	1st Armored Division		11-1-1999	

2nd Cavalry Regiment-Active Component

1-2	Germany	1-8-1951	- -1955
	Fort Meade Maryland	- -1955	- -1958
	Germany	- -1958	7-15-1992
	Fort Lewis Washington	7-15-1992	- -1993
	Fort Polk Louisiana	- -1993	- -2004
	Fort Lewis Washington	- -2004	- -2006

	Germany	Infantry	- -2006	Present
2-2	Germany		1-8-1951	- -1955
	Fort Meade Maryland		- -1955	- -1958
	Germany		- -1958	7-15-1992
	Fort Lewis Washington		7-15-1992	- -1993
	Fort Polk Louisiana		- -1993	- -2004
	Fort Lewis Washington		- -2004	- -2006
	Germany	Infantry	- -2006	Present
3-2	Germany		1-8-1951	- -1955
	Fort Meade Maryland		- -1955	- -1958
	Germany		- -1958	7-15-1992
	Fort Lewis Washington		7-15-1992	- -1993
	Fort Polk Louisiana		- -1993	- -2004
	Fort Lewis Washington		- -2004	- -2006
	Germany	Infantry	- -2006	Present
4-2	Germany		- -1986	7-15-1992
	Fort Lewis Washington		7-15-1992	- -1993
	Fort Polk Louisiana		- -1993	- -2004
	Fort Lewis Washington		- -2004	- -2006
	Germany	RSTA	- -2006	Present
FA SQN	Germany		- -2006	Present
SU SQN	Germany		- -2006	Present

3rd Armored Cavalry Regiment-Active Component

1-3	Fort Meade Maryland	1-8-1951	------------
	Germany	------------	------------
	Fort Lewis Washington	------------	------------
	Fort Meade Maryland	------------	------------
	Fort Bliss Texas	------------	------------
	Fort Carson Colorado	------------	Present
2-3	Fort Meade Maryland	1-8-1951	------------
	Germany	------------	------------
	Fort Lewis Washington	------------	------------
	Fort Meade Maryland	------------	------------
	Fort Bliss Texas	------------	------------
	Fort Carson Colorado	------------	Present
3-3	Fort Meade Maryland	1-8-1951	------------
	Germany	------------	------------
	Fort Lewis Washington	------------	------------

	Fort Meade Maryland		------------	------------
	Fort Bliss Texas		------------	------------
	Fort Carson Colorado		------------	Present
4-3	Fort Bliss Texas		10-16-1988	------------
	Fort Carson Colorado		------------	Present

4th Cavalry Regiment-Active Component

1-4	1st Infantry Division	RSTA	2-15-1957	Present
2-4	1st Cavalry Division		12-1-1957	8-1-1963
	4th Armored Division		8-1-1963	5-10-1971
	1st Armored Division		5-10-1971	9-13-1972
	24th Infantry Division		1-16-1987	2-16-1996
3-4	25th Infantry Division		2-15-1957	3-16-1987
	3rd Infantry Division		6-16-1989	2-16-1996
	25th Infantry Division	RSTA	2-16-1996	Present
4-4	102nd Infantry Division		6-1-1959	12-31-1965
	1st Infantry Division			
D-4	197th Infantry Brigade			
	1st Infantry Division		2-25-2000	
5-4	103rd Infantry Division		6-1-1959	3-1-1963
	1st Infantry Division	RSTA		
E-4	205th Infantry Brigade		1-15-1964	6-5-1994
	1st Infantry Division			
F-4	1st Aviation Brigade		2-10-1971	2-26-1973
	197th Infantry Brigade		- -1990	6-14-1991
	1st Infantry Division		1-16-1999	- -2006
6-4	1st Infantry Division	RSTA	4-17-2007	Present

5th Cavalry Regiment-Active Component

1-5	1st Cavalry Division		10-15-1957	Present
2-5	1st Cavalry Division		8-1-1963	7-31-1972
	1st Cavalry Division		6-20-1974	9-16-1986
	3rd Armored Division		9-16-1986	12-16-1986
	1st Cavalry Division		1-16-1987	Present
3-5	9th Infantry Division		12-1-1957	1-31-1962
	9th Infantry Division		2-1-1966	10-13-1970
	South Vietnam		10-13-1970	11-8-1971
	9th Infantry Division		10-21-1972	3-16-1987

	3rd Armored Division	10-16-1988	8-15-1992
	1st Armored Division	8-15-1992	2-15-1997
4-5	94th Infantry Division	5-1-1959	3-1-1963
D-5	187th Infantry Brigade	1-21-1964	4-15-1994
5-5	81st Infantry Division	4-1-1963	12-31-1965
	3rd Armored Division	10-16-1988	10-16-1991
F-5	2nd Infantry Brigade	2-15-1958	4-13-1962

6th Cavalry Regiment-Active Component

1-6	Fort Knox Kentucky	12-20-1948	10-24-1963
	Fort Meade Maryland	3-25-1967	6-21-1973
	1st Cavalry Division	6-21-1973	2-21-1975
	6th Cavalry Brigade	2-21-1975	--------------
	3rd Corps-Fort Hood Texas	--------------	12-15-1995
	South Korea	7-16-1996	Present
2-6	Fort Knox Kentucky	12-20-1948	10-24-1963
	Fort Meade Maryland	3-23-1967	6-21-1973
	Fort Knox Kentucky	4-1-1974	5-30-1986
	3rd Corps-Fort Hood Texas	7-16-1986	--------------
	11th Aviation Regiment	--------------	6-6-2006
	25th Infantry Division	6-6-2006	Present
3-6	Fort Knox Kentucky	12-20-1948	10-24-1963
	Fort Meade Maryland	3-23-1967	3-31-1971
	3rd Corps-Fort Hood Texas	7-16-1986	12-15-1995
	South Korea	7-16-1996	Present
4-6	5th Corps-Germany	- -1989	12-15-1995
5-6	5th Corps-Germany	- -1989	12-15-1995
6-6	5th Corps-Germany	- -1989	----------------
	11th Aviation Regiment	--------------	
	10th Infantry Division		
7-6	Conroe Texas	- -1989	Present

7th Cavalry Regiment-Active Component

1-7	1st Cavalry Division	11-1-1957	8-22-1972
	1st Cavalry Division	6-20-1974	Present
2-7	3rd Infantry Division	7-1-1957	6-5-1963
	1st Cavalry Division	6-5-1963	1-16-1987
	4th Infantry Division	2-16-1987	12-16-1992
	2nd Armored Division	12-16-1992	8-16-1993
	1st Cavalry Division	8-16-1993	Present

118

3-7	10th Infantry Division		7-1-1957	6-14-1958
	2nd Infantry Division		6-14-1958	2-20-1963
	3rd Infantry Division		6-5-1963	10-16-1986
	8th Infantry Division		12-16-1986	11-16-1992
	3rd Infantry Division		2-16-1996	Present
4-7	2nd Infantry Division		2-20-1963	1-18-1988
	3rd Armored Division		2-16-1989	10-16-1991
	2nd Infantry Division		4-5-1996	Present
5-7	1st Cavalry Division		4-1-1966	3-29-1971
	1st Cavalry Division		9-2-1975	9-30-1976
	3rd Infantry Division		7-21-2004	Present

8th Cavalry Regiment-Active Component

1-8	1st Cavalry Division		12-1-1957	Present
2-8	4th Infantry Division		4-1-1957	9-1-1963
	1st Cavalry Division		9-1-1963	6-28-1972
	1st Cavalry Division		4-20-1974	Present
3-8	8th Infantry Division		8-1-1957	12-16-1986
	3rd Armored Division		2-16-1987	11-15-1991
	1st Cavalry Division		12-16-1992	Present
4-8	96th Infantry Division		6-1-1959	3-15-1963
	3rd Armored Division		2-16-1987	10-16-1991
D-8	191st Infantry Brigade		9-1-1964	2-28-1968
5-8	63rd Infantry Division		6-1-1959	12-31-1965
F-8	23rd Infantry Division		4-1-1968	11-30-1971
	196th Infantry Brigade		11-30-1971	6-29-1972
	1st Aviation Brigade		6-29-1972	2-26-1973
6-8	3rd Infantry Division		6-21-2004	Present

9th Cavalry Regiment-Active Component

1-9	1st Cavalry Division		11-1-1957	10-16-1986
	9th Infantry Division		3-16-1987	2-16-1991
	1st Cavalry Division	RSTA	12-16-1992	Present
A-9	199th Infantry Brigade		2-16-1991	7-16-1992
2-9	9th Infantry Division		12-1-1957	7-1-1958
	24th Infantry Division		7-1-1958	4-15-1970
	24th Infantry Division		9-21-1975	1-16-1987
	7th Infantry Division		3-16-1987	8-15-1993

B-9	4th Infantry Division			
3-9	79th Infantry Division		4-6-1959	2-28-1963
C-9	157th Infantry Brigade		2-1-1964	10-15-1994
4-9	83rd Infantry Division		3-20-1959	12-31-1965
	6th Infantry Division		11-24-1967	7-25-1968
	1st Cavalry Division		5-1-1971	6-30-1971
	1st Cavalry Division		11-19-1974	2-21-1975
	6th Cavalry Brigade		2-21-1975	7-15-1986
	6th Infantry Division		3-16-1987	12-16-1995
	1st Cavalry Division	RSTA	7-18-2005	Present
D-9	1st Cavalry Division		9-30-2002	7-18-2005
5-9	194th Armored Brigade		12-21-1962	1-4-1968
	25th Infantry Division		3-16-1987	8-16-1995
	1st Cavalry Division	RSTA	10-16-2005	Present
E-9	Fort Ord California		1-4-1968	7-1-1973
	3rd Infantry Division			
F-9	1st Cavalry Division		6 30-1971	2-26-1973
	1st Cavalry Division		4-17-2003	7-14-2005
6-9	1st Cavalry Division	RSTA	7-14-2005	Present

10th Cavalry Regiment-Active Component

A-10	Fort Knox Kentucky		6-25-1958	9-1-1963
1-10	4th Infantry Division		9-1-1963	2-16-1987
	194th Armored Brigade		2-16-1987	12-16-1992
	4th Infantry Division		12-16-1992	10-15-1995
	4th Infantry Division	RSTA	3-15-1996	Present
2-10	7th Infantry Division		7-1-1957	4-2-1971
	7th Infantry Division		12-21-1975	2-16-1987
	194th Armored Brigade		6-16-1987	9-16-1990
3-10	77th Infantry Division		6-1-1959	12-31-1965
	1st Cavalry Division		7-1-1977	3-16-1984
C-10	1st Cavalry Division		9-18-2001	7-12-2005
D-10	Fort Knox Kentucky		9-1-1963	4-15-1968
	194th Armored Brigade		4-15-1968	9-16-1990
F-10	5th Infantry Division		11-15-1969	12-15-1970
G-10	4th Infantry Division		9-16-2000	3-11-2005
7-10	4th Infantry Division	RSTA	3-11-2005	Present
H-10	25th Infantry Division		12-6-1969	3-15-1972
	17th Aviation Group		4-30-1972	2-26-1973
	4th Infantry Division		9-16-2000	3-11-2005
8-10	4th Infantry Division	RSTA	3-11-2005	Present

11th Armored Cavalry Regiment-Active Component

1-11	Germany		4-1-1951	8- -1964
	Fort Meade Maryland		8- -1964	9-8-1966
	South Vietnam		9-8-1966	5-17-1972
	Germany		5-17-1972	3-15-1994
	Fort Irwin California	Armor	10-15-1994	Present
2-11	Germany		4-1-1951	8- -1964
	Fort Meade Maryland		8- -1964	9-8-1966
	South Vietnam		9-8-1966	4-6-1971
	Germany		5-17-1972	3-15-1994
	Fort Irwin California	Infantry	10-15-1994	Present
3-11	Germany		4-1-1951	8- -1964
	Fort Meade Maryland		8- -1964	9-8-1966
	South Vietnam		9-8-1966	5-17-1971
	Germany		5-17-1972	3-15-1994
4-11	Germany		- -1985	3-15-1994

12th Cavalry Regiment-Active Component

1-12	1st Armored Division		2-15-1957	4-20-1959
	1st Cavalry Division		9-1-1963	6-15-1983
	Fort Knox Kentucky	T	10-30-1986	9-8-1992
	1st Cavalry Division		12-16-1992	Present
A-12	1st Armored Division		4-20-1959	2-3-1962
2-12	1st Cavalry Division		10-15-1957	9-1-1963
	1st Cavalry Division		7-1-1965	6-29-1972
	1st Cavalry Division		5-21-1975	12-15-1981
	Fort Knox Kentucky	T	10-31-1986	9-8-1992
3-12	3rd Armored Division		10-1-1957	2-16-1989
4-12	5th Infantry Division		2-15-1962	12-15-1970
	4th Infantry Division		12-15-1970	7-31-1972
	5th Infantry Division		5-21-1975	
5-12	90th Infantry Division		3-15-1963	12-31-1965
	Fort Knox Kentucky	T	10-31-1986	9-8-1992
6-12	Fort Knox Kentucky	T	10-31-1986	9-8-1992

13th Cavalry Regiment-Active Component

Unit	Assignment		Start	End
1-13	1st Armored Division		2-15-1957	5-5-1971
	1st Cavalry Division		5-5-1971	6-21-1974
	1st Armored Division		6-21-1974	2-20-1987
	1st Armored Division	RSTA	2-16-1996	Present
2-13	3rd Armored Division		10-1-1957	2-3-1962
	1st Armored Division		2-3-1962	5-5-1971
	1st Cavalry Division		5-5-1971	4-23-1973
	Fort Knox Kentucky	T	3-25-1987	- -1996
C-13	194th Armored Brigade		11-15-1972	- -1974
4-13	Fort Stewart Georgia		7-25-1962	3-26-1963
	Fort Knox Kentucky		3-25-1987	- -1996

14th Cavalry Regiment-Active Component

Unit	Assignment	Start	End
1-14	Germany	12-20-1958	5-17-1972
	2nd Infantry Division	9-15-2000	Present
2-14	Germany	12-20-1948	5-17-1972
	25th Infantry Division	5-16-2002	Present
3-14	Germany	12-20-1948	5-17-1972
4-14	172nd Infantry Brigade	11-21-2003	Present
5-14	25th Infantry Division	10-14-2005	10-16-2006

15th Cavalry Regiment-Active Component

Unit	Assignment		Start	End
1-15	2nd Armored Division		7-1-1957	7-1-1963
	1st Cavalry Division		7-1-1963	7-1-1965
A-15	197th Infantry Brigade		3-21-1973	
2-15	4th Armored Division		4-1-1957	8-1-1963
	1st Cavalry Division		8-1-1963	7-1-1965
3-15	81st Infantry Division		5-1-1959	3-15-1963
	90th Infantry Division		3-15-1963	12-31-1965
4-15	90th Infantry Division		3-15-1963	12-31-1965
E-15	Fort Hood Texas		1-25-1967	7-1-1967
	Fort Campbell Kentucky		7-20-1968	10-25-1968
	Fort Knox Kentucky		2-24-1969	- -1971
5-15	Fort Knox Kentucky	T	3-25-1987	7-10-2007
	194th Armored Brigade	T	7-10-2007	Present
F-15	Fort Hood Texas		1-25-1967	7-1-1967
	Fort Hood Texas		7-20-1968	10-25-1968
	5th Infantry Division		11-15-1969	8-25-1971
G-15	Fort Hood Texas		12-15-1971	1-1-1972

16th Cavalry Regiment-Active Component

1-16	2nd Missile Command		3-1-1957	8-25-1961
	82nd Airborne Division		3-6-1964	8-15-1965
	Fort Knox Kentucky	T	9-8-1992	Present
2-16	1st Missile Command		6-24-1958	6-25-1959
	101st Airborne Division		2-3-1964	5-21-1965
	Fort Knox Kentucky	T	9-8-1992	Present
C-16	1st Aviation Brigade		3-20-1970	2-26-1973
3-16	Fort Knox Kentucky	T	9-8-1992	Present
D-16	173rd Airborne Brigade		6-25-1963	8-28-1968
4-16	Fort Knox Kentucky	T	9-8-1992	
E-16	171st Infantry Brigade		9-22-1969	6-30-1972
5-16	Fort Knox Kentucky	T	9-8-1992	
F-16	172nd Infantry Brigade		9-22-1969	6-30-1972
6-16	Fort Knox Kentucky	T	3-25-1987	9-8-1992

17th Cavalry Regiment-Active Component

A-17	82nd Airborne Division	9-1-1957	5-25-1965
	82nd Airborne Division	5-25-1965	Present
B-17	101st Airborne Division	4-25-1957	2-3-1964
	101st Airborne Division	2-3-1964	Present
C-17	11th Airborne Division	3-1-1957	7-1-1958
	Germany	7-1-1958	11-15-1958
	Fort Knox Kentucky	3-15-1962	1-16-1963
3-17	11th Air Assault Division	3-19-1964	7-1-1965
B-3-17	11th Air Assault Division	2-7-1963	7-1-1965
3-17	Fort Knox Kentucky	11-25-1966	11-30-1967
	South Vietnam	11-30-1967	6-19-1973
	10th Infantry Division	6-2-1988	Present
E-3-17	6th Infantry Division	12-15-1995	4-17-1998
D-17	Fort Rucker Alabama	9-24-1962	2-24-1963
	199th Infantry Brigade	6-1-1966	10-15-1970
4-17	Fort Bragg North Carolina	1-18-1988	1-16-1994
E-17	173rd Airborne Brigade	6-25-1963	1-14-1972
5-17	2nd Infantry Division	1-18-1988	4-5-1996
F-17	196th Infantry Brigade	9-15-1965	2-15-1969
	23rd Infantry Division	2-15-1969	11-30-1971
	196th Infantry Brigade	11-30-1971	3-31-1972

6-17	25th Infantry Division		11-16-2005	Present
7-17	Fort Knox Kentucky		11-25-1966	10-28-1967
	1st Aviation Brigade		10-28-1967	4-18-1972
	1st Cavalry Division		4-18-1972	2-21-1975
	6th Cavalry Brigade		2-21-1975	7-16-1986
	101st Airborne Division			Present
H-17	198th Infantry Brigade		5-10-1967	2-15-1969
	23rd Infantry Division		2-15-1969	10-1-1971
	1st Aviation Brigade		4-30-1972	2-26-1973
I-17				
K-17	82nd Airborne Division		7-15-1968	12-15-1969
	1st Aviation Brigade		10-1-1970	12- -1970

18th Cavalry Regiment-National Guard

1-18	California		3-1-1963	1-13-1974
	40th Infantry Division	RSTA	1-13-1974	Present
G-18	40th Infantry Division			Present
H-18	40th Infantry Division			Present

19th Cavalry Regiment-National Guard

1-19	40th Infantry Division	RSTA		
E-19	29th Infantry Brigade		12-17-1967	9-1-1997

20th Armor Regiment-National Guard

1-20	133rd Armor Group		6-1-1961	12-17-1967
2-20	133rd Armor Group		6-1-1961	12-17-1967
3-20	133rd Armor Group		6-1-1961	12-17-1967
4-20	133rd Armor Group		6-1-1961	12-17-1967

26th Cavalry Regiment-National Guard

1-26	26th Infantry Division		3-1-1963	4-1-1988

32nd Cavalry Regiment-Active Component

1-32	3rd Armored Division		10-1-1957	6-16-1986
	1st Cavalry Division		10-16-1986	12-16-1992

	2nd Infantry Division		4-16-1995	9-15-2000
	101st Airborne Division	RSTA	9-16-2004	Present
2-32	1st Armored Division		2-15-1957	12-23-1957
	3rd Armored Division		2-3-1962	8-15-1991
	1st Armored Division		8-15-1991	10-16-1992
3-32	Fort Stewart Georgia		6-25-1958	9-1-1963
	3rd Armored Division		9-1-1963	6-16-1986
	1st Cavalry Division		10-16-1986	12-16-1992
4-32	Jefferson City Indiana		6-1-1959	1-31-1968
	3rd Armored Division		12-16-1986	12-15-1991
5-32	Germany		9-1-1963	5-1-1966
	24th Infantry Division		5-1-1966	11-16-1987
6-32	Fort Knox Kentucky		11-25-1966	9-13-1972
	4th Infantry Division		9-13-1972	4-1-1984

33rd Cavalry Regiment-Active Component

1-33	3rd Armored Division		10-1-1957	2-16-1987
	Fort Lewis Washington		4-16-1987	8-15-1988
	9th Infantry Division		8-15-1988	9-28-1990
	199th Infantry Brigade		2-16-1991	7-16-1992
	Fort Polk Louisiana		7-16-1992	1-14-1994
	2nd Infantry Division		4-16-1995	9-15-2000
	25th Infantry Division		9-15-2000	5-16-2002
	101st Airborne Division	RSTA	9-16-2004	Present
2-33	1st Armored Division		2-15-1957	12-23-1957
	Germany		5-1-1958	10-1-1963
	3rd Armored Division		10-1-1963	9-16-1986
	1st Cavalry Division		9-16-1986	10-16-1986
	Fort Knox Kentucky		12-16-1992	10-16-1995
3-33	Fort Knox Kentucky		6-25-1958	7-1-1963
	3rd Armored Division		7-1-1963	2-16-1987
4-33	103rd Infantry Division		5-18-1959	2-15-1963
	205th Infantry Brigade		2-15-1963	1-31-1968
5-33	Fort Knox Kentucky		7-1-1963	4-15-1968
	194th Armored Brigade		4-15-1968	6-16-1986

34th Armor Regiment-Active Component

1-34	4th Infantry Division	4-1-1957	10-15-1965
	1st Infantry Division	8-1-1979	
2-34	Fort Ord California	6-1-1957	4-25-1961
	4th Infantry Division	10-1-1963	8-1-1967
	25th Infantry Division	8-1-1967	12-15-1970
	4th Infantry Division	12-15-1970	7-14-1987
	1st Infantry Division	2-16-1988	
	1st Armored Division		
3-34	24th Infantry Division	7-1-1958	2-1-1963
	1st Infantry Division	2-16-1988	7-15-1991
D-34	Fort Kobbe Canal Zone	11-15-1957	8-8-1962
4-34	8th Infantry Division	2-16-1988	1-17-1992
E-34	Fort Sill Oklahoma	1-22-1958	3-25-1961
F-34	2nd Infantry Brigade	2-15-1958	2-19-1962
G-34	2nd Infantry Brigade	2-15-1958	4-20-1962
H-34	Fort Knox Kentucky	6-25-1958	12-12-1958
8-34	Fort Knox Kentucky	12-12-1958	9-24-1963
9-34	94th Infantry Division	5-1-1959	1-7-1963
	187th Infantry Brigade	1-7-1963	1-31-1968

35th Armor Regiment-Active Component

1-35	4th Armored Division	4-1-1957	5-10-1971
	1st Armored Division	5-10-1971	10-16-1991
	1st Armored Division	2-15-1997	Present
2-35	2nd Armored Division	4-1-1957	7-1-1963
	4th Infantry Division	11-16-1988	1-16-1996
3-35	Germany	5-1-1958	6-5-1963
	4th Armored Division	6-5-1963	5-10-1971
	1st Armored Division	5-10-1971	10-16-1991
4-35	102nd Infantry Division	6-1-1959	4-1-1963
	4th Armored Division	7-1-1963	5-10-1971
	1st Armored Division	5-10-1971	
	5th Infantry Division	11-16-1988	11-24-1992
5-35	Albuquerque New Mexico	6-1-1959	1-1-1966
	Laredo Texas	1-1-1966	1-31-1968
6-35	102nd Infantry Division	4-1-1963	12-31-1965
7-35	102nd Infantry Division	4-1-1963	12-31-1965

37th Armor Regiment-Active Component

1-37	4th Armored Division	4-1-1957	5-5-1971
	1st Armored Division	5-5-1971	1-17-1992
	3rd Infantry Division	1-17-1992	2-16-1996
	1st Armored Division	2-17-1997	Present
2-37	2nd Armored Division	7-1-1957	7-1-1963
	4th Armored Division	7-1-1963	5-10-1971
	1st Armored Division	5-10-1971	2-28-1983
	1st Infantry Division	2-28-1983	2-16-1988
	1st Armored Division	4-14-1988	1-17-1992
	3rd Infantry Division	1-17-1992	2-15-1996
	1st Armored Division	2-17-1997	
3-37	Germany	7-1-1957	6-17-1963
	4th Armored Division	6-17-1963	5-5-1971
	1st Armored Division	5-5-1971	4-20-1974
	1st Infantry Division	2-23-1983	2-16-1996
D-37	Fort Knox Kentucky	6-25-1958	12-12-1958
4-37	Fort Knox Kentucky	12-12-1958	4-15-1968
	194th Armored Brigade	4-15-1968	2-23-1983
	1st Infantry Division	2-23-1983	2-16-1996
	1st Armored Division		Present
5-37	90th Infantry Division	4-1-1959	3-27-1963

40th Armor Regiment-Active Component

A-40	Ladd AFB Alaska	12-16-1957	5-20-1963
	171st Infantry Brigade	5-20-1963	9-21-1969
1-40	5th Infantry Division	6-21-1976	12-16-1986
	Fort Hunter Liggert California	1-16-1996	3-15-1997
	25th Infantry Division	10-16-2005	Present
B-40	Fort Sill Oklahoma	10-24-1963	- -1976
2-40	7th Infantry Division	7-1-1957	7-1-1963
3-40	1st Cavalry Division	12-1-1957	7-15-1963
	South Korea	7-15-1963	9-1-1963
D-40	Fort Richardson Alaska	12-16-1957	7-1-1963
	172nd Infantry Brigade	7-1-1963	9-21-1969
4-40	4th Infantry Division	3-1-1976	4-1-1984
5-40	Fort Irwin California	6-25-1958	2-19-1962
	63rd Infantry Division	4-1-1963	12-31-1965

F-40	Berlin Germany		6-1-1958	9-1-1963
	Berlin Brigade		9-1-1963	9-16-1990
6-40	Berlin Brigade		9-16-1990	10-15-1994
7-40	63rd Infantry Division		5-1-1959	12-31-1965
8-40	96th Infantry Division		6-1-1959	2-15-1963
	191st Infantry Brigade		2-15-1963	2-28-1968
	Tucson Arizona		2-28-1968	9-15-1996

43rd Cavalry Regiment-National Guard

E-43	Quonset Point Rhode Island		2-1-1968	4-1-1971

50th Armor Regiment-National Guard

1-50	50th Armored Division		3-1-1959	12-1-1971
2-50	50th Armored Division		3-1-1959	12-1-1971
3-50	50th Armored Division		3-1-1959	12-1-1971
4-50	50th Armored Division		3-1-1959	2-1-1968
5-50	50th Armored Division		3-1-1959	1-25-1963
6-50	50th Armored Division		1-25-1963	2-1-1968

53rd Armor Regiment-National Guard

1-53	103rd Armor Group		3-1-1959	4-1-1964
2-53	103rd Armor Group		3-1-1959	4-1-1964

61st Cavalry Regiment-Active Component

1-61	101st Airborne Division	RSTA	9-16-2004	Present
2-61	4th Infantry Division	RSTA		

63rd Armor Regiment-Active Component

1-63	1st Infantry Division		7-1-1963	8-16-1987
	Fort Irwin California		9-16-1987	10-16-1991
	177th Armored Brigade		10-16-1991	10-15-1994
	1st Infantry Division		2-16-1996	- -2006
2-63	1st Infantry Division		1-2-1964	9-15-1965
	1st Infantry Division		4-15-1970	2-23-1983
	1st Infantry Division		2-16-1996	- -2006

3-63	1st Infantry Division	4-15-1970	8-1-1979
	3rd Infantry Division	8-1-1979	11-16-1987
4-63	1st Infantry Division	4-15-1970	2-23-1983

64th Armor Regiment-Active Component

1-64	3rd Infantry Division	4-1-1963	11-16-1987
	24th Infantry Division	11-16-1987	2-16-1996
	3rd Infantry Division	2-16-1996	Present
2-64	3rd Infantry Division	6-17-1963	2-16-1996
3-64	3rd Infantry Division	6-17-1963	2-16-1996
4-64	3rd Infantry Division	5-1-1966	
	24th Infantry Division	8-15-1983	2-16-1996
	3rd Infantry Division	2-16-1996	Present

66th Armor Regiment-Active Component

1-66	2nd Armored Division	7-1-1957	- -1990
	2nd Armored Division	12-16-1992	1-16-1996
	4th Infantry Division	1-16-1996	Present
2-66	4th Armored Division	4-1-1957	7-1-1963
	2nd Armored Division	7-1-1963	4-15-1992
C-66	1st Infantry Brigade	9-24-1959	9-20-1962
3-66	Fort Benning Georgia	6-25-1958	6-25-1959
	Fort Hood Texas	8-12-1963	10-15-1965
	2nd Armored Division	9-1-1980	4-15-1992
	2nd Armored Division	12-16-1992	1-16-1996
	4th Infantry Division	1-16-1996	
D-66	Fort Campbell Kentucky	6-22-1958	7-25-1965
4-66	3rd Infantry Division	4-16-1986	1-17-1992
5-66	Rockville Maryland	5-15-1959	1-31-1968
6-66	77th Infantry Division	3-26-1963	12-31-1965
7-66	77th Infantry Division	3-26-1963	12-31-1965

67th Armor Regiment-Active Component

1-67	2nd Armored Division	7-1-1957	5-21-1991
	1st Cavalry Division	5-21-1991	12-16-1992
	2nd Armored Division	12-16-1992	1-16-1996
	4th Infantry Division	1-16-1996	Present

2-67	4th Armored Division	4-1-1957	7-1-1963
	2nd Armored Division	7-1-1963	10-1-1983
	3rd Armored Division	6-16-1986	10-16-1991
	1st Armored Division	10-16-1991	2-15-1997
3-67	Tallahassee Florida	6-1-1959	5-1-1964
	2nd Armored Division	3-1-1975	5-21-1991
	1st Cavalry Division	5-21-1991	8-16-1993
	2nd Armored Division	8-16-1993	1-16-1996
	4th Infantry Division	1-16-1996	
4-67	Wheeling West Virginia	4-17-1959	2-15-1968
	3rd Armored Division	6-16-1986	10-16-1991
	1st Armored Division	10-16-1991	2-15-1997
5-67	Tallahassee Florida	5-1-1964	1-31-1968

68th Armor Regiment-Active Component

1-68	3rd Infantry Division	7-1-1957	4-1-1963
	8th Infantry Division	4-1-1963	3-15-1991
	4th Infantry Division	1-16-1996	Present
2-68	8th Infantry Division	7-1-1957	1-17-1992
	1st Armored Division	1-17-1992	2-15-1997
3-68	9th Infantry Division	12-1-1957	1-31-1962
	8th Infantry Division	4-1-1963	4-1-1984
	4th Infantry Division	4-1-1984	1-16-1996
4-68	Fort Bragg North Carolina	6-13-1958	7-1-1965
	Fort Stewart Georgia	7-1-1965	6-16-1969
	82nd Airborne Division	6-16-1969	2-14-1984
	4th Infantry Division	4-1-1984	12-15-1989
5-68	77th Infantry Division	6-1-1959	3-26-1963
	8th Infantry Division	4-1-1966	4-1-1984
6-68	79th Infantry Division	4-20-1959	1-7-1963
	Bethlehem Pennsylvania	1-7-1963	1-31-1968
	157th Infantry Brigade	1-31-1968	10-15-1994
7-68	83rd Infantry Division	3-20-1959	12-31-1965
	83rd Infantry Division	4-1-1963	12-31-1965

69th Armor Regiment-Active Component

1-69	1st Infantry Division	2-15-1957	7-1-1963
	25th Infantry Division	7-1-1963	8-1-1967

	4th Infantry Division		8-1-1967	12-15-1970
	25th Infantry Division		12-15-1970	6-5-1972
	3rd Infantry Division		11-16-1987	1-17-1992
2-69	10th Infantry Division		7-1-1957	6-14-1958
	2nd Infantry Division		6-14-1958	3-1-1963
	197th Infantry Brigade		3-21-1973	6-15-1991
	24th Infantry Division		6-15-1991	2-16-1996
	3rd Infantry Division		2-16-1996	Present
3-69	25th Infantry Division		2-15-1957	7-1-1963
	24th Infantry Division		11-16-1987	2-16-1996
	3rd Infantry Division		2-16-1996	Present
D-69	1st Infantry Brigade		7-25-1958	9-20-1962
4-69	197th Infantry Brigade		9-20-1962	6-30-1971
	8th Infantry Division		9-21-1972	8-1-1984
	3rd Infantry Division		11-16-1987	1-17-1992
5-69	81st Infantry Division		5-1-1959	12-31-1965
6-69	81st Infantry Division		4-1-1963	12-31-1965
H-69	197th Infantry Brigade		6-30-1971	3-21-1973

70th Armor Regiment-Active Component

1-70	24th Infantry Division		2-1-1963	4-15-1970
	4th Infantry Division		9-13-1972	6-16-1986
	5th Infantry Division		12-16-1986	11-24-1992
	194th Armored Brigade			1-16-1996
2-70	24th Infantry Division		2-1-1963	4-15-1970
	24th Infantry Division		6-21-1977	10-16-1987
	1st Armored Division		12-16-1987	1-17-1992
	3rd Infantry Division		1-17-1992	12-15-1993
	1st Armored Division		2-16-1996	Present
3-70	24th Infantry Division		2-1-1963	4-15-1970
	5th Infantry Division		6-21-1977	11-24-1992
4-70	Fort Knox Kentucky		4-15-1970	10- -1970
	5th Infantry Division		10- -1970	12-15-1970
	4th Infantry Division		12-15-1970	9-13-1972
	1st Armored Division		12-16-1986	1-17-1992

71st Cavalry Regiment-Active Component

1-71	10th Infantry Division	RSTA	9-16-2004	Present
2-71	10th Infantry Division	RSTA		

3-71	10th Infantry Division	RSTA	9-16-2004	Present

72nd Armor Regiment-Active Component

1-72	2nd Infantry Division		3-1-1963	
2-72	2nd Infantry Division		3-25-1963	6-27-1971
	2nd Infantry Division		10-21-1978	Present

73rd Armor Regiment-Active Component

1-73	7th Infantry Division		7-1-1963	4-2-1971
	2nd Infantry Division		4-2-1971	8-14-1971
	NTC-Fort Irwin California		10-1-1981	8-16-1987
	82nd Airborne Division	RSTA		Present
3-73	82nd Airborne Division		2-14-1984	7-15-1997
	82nd Airborne Division	RSTA		Present
4-73	194th Armored Brigade		12-21-1962	1-4-1968
	3rd Infantry Division		9-21-1972	2-23-1983
	82nd Airborne Division	RSTA		Present
D-73	Fort Ord California		1-4-1968	3-20-1970
5-73	194th Armored Brigade		2-23-1983	6-16-1987
	82nd Airborne Division	RSTA		Present

75th Cavalry Regiment-Active Component

1-75	101st Airborne Division	RSTA	9-16-2004	Present

77th Armor Regiment-Active Component

1-77	5th Infantry Division		2-19-1962	8-27-1971
	4th Infantry Division		3-21-1973	12-15-1989
	1st Infantry Division		2-16-1996	Present
2-77	5th Infantry Division		2-19-1962	10-1-1963
	9th Infantry Division		8-21-1977	6-16-1986
	4th Infantry Division		6-16-1986	1-16-1996
3-77	5th Infantry Division		2-19-1962	12-15-1970
	5th Infantry Division		6-21-1977	6-16-1986
	8th Infantry Division		6-16-1986	1-17-1992
	1st Armored Division		1-17-1992	4-16-1995
4-77	157th Infantry Brigade		1-17-1963	1-31-1968

5-77	8th Infantry Division		4-1-1984	1-17-1992
	1st Armored Division		1-17-1992	4-16-1995

81st Armor Regiment-Active Component

1-81	1st Armored Division		2-3-1962	5-5-1971
	1st Cavalry Division		5-5-1971	7-20-1974
	Fort Knox Kentucky	T	3-25-1987	7-10-2007
	194th Armored Brigade	T	7-10-2007	Present
2-81	1st Armored Division		2-3-1962	3-1-1971
	1st Armored Division		9-13-1972	6-16-1989
	Fort Knox Kentucky	T	1-16-1996	7-10-2007
	194th Armored Brigade	T	7-10-2007	Present
3-81	Fort Knox Kentucky	T	3-25-1987	10-1-1991
	Fort Knox Kentucky	T	9-30-1993	7-10-2007
	194th Armored Brigade	T	7-10-2007	Present
4-81	Salt Lake City Utah		3-15-1963	8-10-1963
	191st Infantry Brigade		8-10-1963	2-28-1968

82nd Cavalry Regiment-National Guard

1-82	41st Infantry Division		4-1-1959	3-1-1968
	116th Cavalry Brigade	INF	9-1-1989	9-1-1997
	40th Infantry Division	RSTA		
HHC	Bend Oregon		9-1-1997	
E-82	41st Infantry Brigade		3-1-1968	9-1-1989
	41st Infantry Brigade		9-1-1997	
F-82	29th Infantry Brigade		9-1-1997	
G-82	116th Cavalry Brigade		9-1-1997	

86th Cavalry Regiment-National Guard

E-86	86th Armored Brigade		2-1-1964	2-1-1968

89th Cavalry Regiment-Active Component

1-89	10th Infantry Division	RSTA		Present
3-89	10th Infantry Division			Present

91st Cavalry Regiment-Active Component

1-91	173rd Airborne Brigade			Present

94th Cavalry Regiment-National Guard

1-94	47th Infantry Division	CAV	4-1-1963	2-1-1968
	47th Infantry Division	ARM	1-1-1972	2-10-1991
	34th Infantry Division		2-10-1991	9-1-2002

98th Cavalry Regiment-National Guard

1-98	31st Infantry Division		5-1-1963	2-15-1968
	36th Infantry Division	RSTA		
A-98	155th Armored Brigade		11-1-1973	
D-98	Mississippi		2-15-1968	11-1-1973

101st Cavalry Regiment-National Guard

1-101	42nd Infantry Division		3-16-1959
2-101	42nd Infantry Division	RSTA	
E-101	27th Infantry Brigade		9-1-1996

102nd Armored Cavalry Regiment-National Guard

1-102	New Jersey		3-1-1959	2-1-1968
2-102	New Jersey		3-1-1959	2-1-1968
3-102	Vermont		3-1-1959	4-1-1964
	New Jersey		4-1-1964	2-1-1968

102nd Cavalry Regiment-National Guard

1-102	102nd Armor Group		2-1-1968	7-1-1975
	50th Armored Division		7-1-1975	9-1-1991
	42nd Infantry Division	RSTA		
2-102	102nd Armor Group		2-1-1968	7-1-1975
	50th Armored Division		7-1-1975	9-1-1993
	42nd Infantry Division		9-1-1993	
3-102	50th Armored Division		12-1-1971	9-1-1993
	42nd Infantry Division		9-1-1993	9-1-1994
4-102	50th Armored Division		12-1-1971	7-1-1975
5-102	50th Armored Division		12-1-1971	9-1-1991

103rd Armored Cavalry Regiment-National Guard

1-103	Maine		3-1-1959	6-1-1961
2-103	Maine		3-1-1959	6-1-1961
3-103	Maine		3-1-1959	6-1-1961

103rd Armor Regiment-National Guard

1-103	28th Infantry Division		6-1-1959	
2-103	28th Infantry Division		6-1-1959	2-17-1968
	28th Infantry Division		3-1-1992	
3-103	Attached-104th Armd Cav Regt		5-1-1962	4-1-1963
	Attached-28th Infantry Division		2-17-1968	1-1-1976
4-103	28th Infantry Division			

104th Cavalry Regiment-National Guard

1-104	Pennsylvania	ACR	9-1-1950	4-1-1975
	28th Infantry Division	RSTA	4-1-1975	Present
2-104	Pennsylvania	ACR	9-1-1950	4-1-1975
	28th Infantry Division	RSTA	5-1-2003	Present
3-104	Pennsylvania	ACR	9-23-1953	2-1-1968
	New Jersey	ACR	2-1-1968	6-1-1975
I-104	28th Infantry Division		10-1-2001	
K-104	28th Infantry Division		10-1-2001	

105th Cavalry Regiment-National Guard

1-105	32nd Infantry Division		2-15-1959	12-30-1967
	34th Infantry Division	RSTA		
2-105	32nd Infantry Division		2-15-1959	4-15-1963
E-105	32nd Infantry Brigade		12-30-1967	9-1-1997
	32nd Infantry Brigade		9-1-2001	

106th Cavalry Regiment-National Guard

1-106	33rd Infantry Division		3-1-1959	2-1-1968
2-106	33rd Infantry Division		3-1-1959	4-1-1963
	35th Infantry Division	RSTA		
E-106	33rd Infantry Brigade		2-1-1968	9-1-1995

107th Cavalry Regiment-National Guard

1-107	Ohio	ACR	9-15-1949	5-1-1977
	28th Infantry Division		9-1-1993	9-1-1994
	38th Infantry Division		9-1-1994	9-1-2002
	28th Infantry Division		9-1-2002	
2-107	Ohio	ACR	9-15-1949	9-1-1993
	Kettering Ohio		3-31-1994	9-1-1994
	38th Infantry Division		9-1-1994	
	28th Infantry Division	RSTA		
3-107	Ohio	ACR	9-15-1949	5-1-1968
	West Virginia		5-1-1968	6-1-1974
	Ohio		6-1-1974	9-1-1993

108th Armored Cavalry Regiment-National Guard

1-108	Mississippi	9-1-1959	9-2-1995
2-108	Mississippi	9-1-1959	2-15-1968
3-108	Mississippi	9-1-1959	2-15-1968

108th Armored Regiment-National Guard

1-108	48th Armored Division	7-1-1959	1-1-1968
	30th Armored Division	1-1-1968	11-30-1973
	48th Infantry Brigade	11-30-1973	
2-108	48th Armored Division	7-1-1959	1-1-1968
3-108	48th Armored Division	7-1-1959	1-1-1968
4-108	48th Armored Division	7-1-1959	1-1-1968
5-108	Attached-108th Artillery Brigade	5-1-1962	4-15-1963
	48th Armored Division	4-15-1963	1-1-1968

108th Cavalry Regiment-National Guard

A-108	256th Infantry Brigade		9-2-1995
1-108	35th Infantry Division	RSTA	
2-108	36th Infantry Division	RSTA	
E-108	48th Infantry Brigade		9-2-1995

109th Cavalry Regiment-National Guard

1-109	30th Armored Division	3-1-1959	2-1-1968
2-109	30th Armored Division	3-1-1959	2-1-1968

3-109	30th Armored Division		3-1-1959	2-1-1968
	30th Armored Brigade		11-1-1973	9-1-1995
	38th Infantry Division	RSTA		
4-109	30th Armored Division		3-1-1959	11-1-1973
	30th Armored Brigade		11-1-1973	9-1-1995
5-109	30th Armored Division		3-1-1959	11-1-1973

110th Cavalry Regiment-National Guard

1-110	26th Infantry Division	5-1-1959	9-1-1993
	26th Infantry Brigade	9-1-1993	9-1-1996
2-110	26th Infantry Division	5-1-1959	12-19-1967

111th Cavalry Regiment-National Guard

1-111	40th Armored Division	3-1-1963	1-29-1968
E-111	29th Infantry Brigade	11-1-1965	12-17-1967
	40th Infantry Brigade	1-29-1968	1-13-1974

112th Cavalry Regiment-National Guard

1-112	49th Armored Division		3-16-1959	1-15-1968
	72nd Infantry Brigade		1-15-1968	11-1-1973
	49th Armored Division		11-1-1973	5-1-2004
	36th Infantry Division		5-1-2004	
2-112	49th Armored Division		3-16-1959	1-15-1968
	49th Armor Group		1-15-1968	9-1-1971
	49th Armor Brigade		9-1-1971	11-1-1973
	49th Armored Division		11-1-1973	5-1-2004
	36th Infantry Division		5-1-2004	
3-112	49th Armored Division		3-16-1959	1-15-1968
	49th Armor Group		1-15-1968	9-1-1971
	49th Armor Brigade		9-1-1971	11-1-1973
	49th Armored Division		11-1-1973	5-1-2004
	36th Infantry Division	RSTA	5-1-2004	Present
4-112	49th Armored Division		3-16-1959	1-15-1968
	49th Armored Division		11-1-1973	5-1-2004
	36th Infantry Division		5-1-2004	
5-112	49th Armored Division		3-16-1959	1-15-1968
	49th Armored Division		1-15-1968	5-1-2004

	36th Infantry Division		5-1-2004	
6-112	36th Infantry Division		3-1-1963	1-15-1968
	49th Armored Division		11-1-1973	9-1-1997
7-112	36th Infantry Division		3-1-1963	1-15-1968
	50th Armored Division		6-1-1988	9-1-1993
8-112	50th Armored Division		6-1-1988	9-1-1993

113th Cavalry Regiment-National Guard

1-113	34th Infantry Division		5-1-1959	4-1-1963
	Burlington Iowa		4-1-1963	12-1-1967
	34th Infantry Division	RSTA	9-1-1993	Present
2-113	34th Infantry Division		5-1-1959	4-1-1963
	Knoxville Iowa		4-1-1963	12-1-1967
G-113	34th Infantry Division		9-1-2001	

114th Cavalry Regiment-National Guard

E-114	69th Infantry Brigade		2-14-1964	10-1-1985

115th Armored Regiment-National Guard

1-115	29th Infantry Division		3-1-1959	2-1-1968

116th Armored Regiment-National Guard

1-116	29th Infantry Division		4-1-1963	2-1-1968

116th Cavalry Regiment-National Guard

1-116	Idaho	ACR	9-12-1949	5-1-1977
2-116	Idaho	ACR	9-12-1949	9-1-1989
	116th Cavalry Brigade	ARM	9-1-1989	
	34th Infantry Division	RSTA		
3-116	Idaho	ACR	9-12-1949	12-15-1967
	Nevada	ACR	12-15-1967	4-1-1974
	Oregon	ACR	4-1-1974	9-1-1989
	116th Cavalry Brigade	ARM	9-1-1989	
E-116	41st Infantry Brigade	CAV	9-1-1989	9-1-1997
F-116	116th Cavalry Brigade	CAV	9-1-1989	9-1-1997

138

117th Cavalry Regiment-National Guard

5-117	50th Armored Division		1-25-1963	9-1-1993
	42nd Infantry Division		9-1-1993	

118th Cavalry Regiment-National Guard

E-118	Tucson Arizona		9-1-1996	9-1-1998

121st Cavalry Regiment-National Guard

1-121	27th Armored Division		3-16-1959	2-1-1968

123rd Armored Regiment-National Guard

1-123	149th Armor Group		10-1-1959	11-1-1980
	149th Armored Brigade		11-1-1980	11-1-1985
	35th Infantry Division		11-1-1985	9-1-2002
2-123	149th Armor Group		10-1-1959	11-1-1980
	149th Armored Brigade		11-1-1980	11-1-1985
	35th Infantry Division		11-1-1985	
3-123	149th Armor Group		10-1-1959	3-1-1968
	Fort Knox Kentucky		10-21-1988	6-1-1989

124th Cavalry Regiment-National Guard

1-124	36th Infantry Division		3-16-1959	1-15-1968
	49th Armored Division		1-1-1973	5-1-2004
	36th Infantry Division	RSTA	5-1-2004	Present
2-124	36th Infantry Division		3-16-1959	3-15-1963
	49th Armored Division		3-15-1963	1-15-1968
A-124	71st Airborne Brigade		1-15-1968	11-1-1973
E-124	36th Infantry Brigade		1-15-1968	11-1-1973
F-124	72nd Infantry Brigade		1-15-1968	11-1-1973
G-124	49th Armored Division		10-1-2001	5-1-2004
	36th Infantry Division		5-1-2004	
H-124	49th Armored Division		10-1-2001	5-1-2004
	36th Infantry Division		5-1-2004	
I-124	49th Armored Division		10-1-2001	5-1-2001
	36th Infantry Division		5-1-2001	

125th Armored Regiment-National Guard

1-125	92nd Infantry Brigade		2-15-1959	5-1-1964

126th Cavalry Regiment-National Guard

1-126	33rd Infantry Division		4-1-1963	2-1-1968
	38th Infantry Division	RSTA	10-1-1999	Present
2-126	33rd Infantry Division		4-1-1963	2-1-1968

127th Armored Regiment-National Guard

1-127	27th Armored Division		3-16-1959	2-1-1968
	50th Armored Division		2-1-1968	4-1-1975
	42nd Infantry Division		4-1-1975	
2-127	27th Armored Division		4-15-1963	2-1-1968

131st Cavalry Regiment-National Guard

1-131	231st Armor Group		5-2-1959	1-15-1968
	30th Armored Division		1-15-1968	11-1-1973
	31st Armored Brigade		11-1-1973	9-1-2000
	Ozark Alabama		9-1-2000	9-1-2002
	35th Infantry Division		9-1-2002	
	38th Infantry Division	RSTA		

134th Cavalry Regiment-National Guard

1-134	40th Infantry Division	RSTA		

137th Armored Regiment-National Guard

1-137	37th Infantry Division		9-1-1959	2-1-1968
2-137	37th Infantry Division		9-1-1959	2-1-1968

138th Armored Regiment-National Guard

1-138	38th Infantry Division		2-1-1959	2-1-1968
2-138	38th Infantry Division		2-1-1959	2-1-1968

139th Armored Regiment-National Guard

1-139	39th Infantry Division	7-1-1959	12-1-1967

140th Cavalry Regiment-National Guard

E-140	40th Infantry Brigade	1-29-1968	1-13-1974

142nd Armored Regiment-National Guard

1-142	42nd Infantry Division	3-16-1959	4-1-1975
2-145	42nd Infantry Division	3-16-1959	2-1-1968

145th Cavalry Regiment-National Guard

1-145	45th Infantry Division	4-1-1963	1-2-1968
E-145	45th Infantry Brigade	1-2-1968	

146th Cavalry Regiment-National Guard

1-146	46th Infantry Division	3-15-1959	2-1-1968

147th Armored Regiment-National Guard

1-147	28th Infantry Division	9-1-1993	1-1-1994
	38th Infantry Division	1-1-1994	1-16-2004

149th Armored Regiment-National Guard

1-149	49th Infantry Division	5-1-1959	1-29-1968
	111th Armor Group	1-29-1968	10-1-1971
	California	10-1-1971	1-13-1974
	40th Infantry Division	1-13-1974	
2-149	49th Infantry Division	5-1-1959	3-1-1963
3-149	49th Infantry Division	3-1-1963	1-29-1968
4-149	California	4-1-1964	1-29-1968

150th Cavalry Regiment-National Guard

1-150	West Virginia	ACR	8-1-1955	2-1-1968
	West Virginia	ACR	7-1-1974	9-1-1993
	28th Infantry Division	ARM	9-1-1993	9-1-2002
	30th Armored Brigade	ARM	9-1-2002	
	29th Infantry Division	RSTA		
2-150	West Virginia	ACR	8-1-1955	2-1-1968
3-150	West Virginia	ACR	8-1-1955	2-1-1968

151st Cavalry Regiment-National Guard

1-151	36th Infantry Division	RSTA		
E-151	39th Infantry Brigade		12-1-1967	

152nd Armored Regiment-National Guard

1-152	Alabama		5-2-1959	4-15-1963
	31st Infantry Division		4-15-1963	1-15-1968
	30th Armored Division		1-15-1968	11-1-1973
	31st Armored Brigade		11-1-1973	9-1-2000
2-152	231st Armor Group		4-15-1963	1-15-1968
	Oneonta Alabama		1-15-1968	
3-152	231st Armor Group		4-30-1964	1-15-1968

153rd Cavalry Regiment-National Guard

1-153	28th Infantry Division	RSTA		
E-153	53rd Armored Brigade		3-1-1964	1-20-1968
	53rd Infantry Brigade		1-20-1968	

156th Armored Regiment-National Guard

1-156	256th Infantry Brigade		3-1-1977
	36th Infantry Division		

158th Cavalry Regiment-National Guard

A-158	58th Infantry Brigade		4-1-1975	10-1-1975
B-158	58th Infantry Brigade		4-1-1975	7-1-1986
1-158	29th Infantry Division	RSTA	7-1-1986	Present

163rd Cavalry Regiment-National Guard

1-163	Montana	ACR	3-1-1953	12-1-1988
	163rd Armored Brigade	ARM	12-1-1988	9-1-1997
2-163	Montana	ACR	3-1-1953	12-1-1988
	163rd Armored Brigade	ARM	9-1-1989	9-1-1997
	40th Infantry Division	ARM	9-1-1997	9-1-1998
3-163	Montana	ACR	3-1-1953	2-1-1968
	Oregon	ACR	2-1-1968	8-1-1974
	Nevada	ACR	8-1-1974	4-1-1980
	Texas	ACR	4-1-1980	6-1-1988
E-163	163rd Armored Brigade	CAV	12-1-1988	9-1-1997
	11th Armored Cavalry	CAV	10-1-2000	Present

167th Cavalry Regiment-National Guard

1-167	35th Infantry Division		10-1-1985	
E-167	67th Infantry Brigade		3-1-1964	10-1-1985

170th Cavalry Regiment-National Guard

1-170	49th Infantry Division		3-1-1963	1-29-1968
C-170	49th Infantry Brigade		1-29-1968	5-1-1968
E-170	49th Infantry Brigade		1-29-1968	1-13-1974

172nd Cavalry Regiment-National Guard

1-172	43rd Infantry Division		5-1-1959	4-1-1963
	86th Infantry Brigade		4-1-1963	2-1-1964
	86th Armored Brigade		2-1-1964	2-1-1968
	50th Armored Division		2-1-1968	2-1-1988
	26th Infantry Division		2-1-1988	9-1-1993
	42nd Infantry Division		9-1-1993	
2-172	43rd Infantry Division		5-1-1959	4-1-1963
	86th Infantry Brigade		4-1-1963	2-1-1964
	86th Armored Brigade		2-1-1964	2-1-1968
	50th Armored Division		2-1-1968	2-1-1988
	26th Infantry Division		2-1-1988	9-1-1993
	42nd Infantry Division	RSTA	9-1-1993	Present
3-172	Vermont		2-1-1964	4-1-1966
	Attached-86th Armored Brigade		4-1-1966	2-1-1968

174th Armored Regiment-National Guard

1-174	27th Armored Division	3-16-1959	10-1-1960
	Niagara Falls New York	10-1-1960	3-1-1964
	27th Armored Division	3-1-1964	2-1-1968

182nd Cavalry Regiment-National Guard

| 1-182 | 42nd Infantry Division | RSTA | |

183rd Cavalry Regiment-National Guard

1-183	29th Infantry Division	3-1-1959	2-1-1968
2-183	29th Infantry Division	2-11-2006	Present
C-183	116th infantry Brigade	4-1-1975	6-1-1986

185th Armored Regiment-National Guard

1-185	40th Armored Division	7-1-1959	1-29-1968
	40th Armored Brigade	1-29-1968	1-13-1974
	40th Infantry Division	1-13-1974	9-1-1999
	81st Infantry Brigade	9-1-1999	8-1-2000
	81st Armored Brigade	8-1-2000	
	40th Infantry Division		
2-185	40th Armored Division	7-1-1959	1-29-1968
	40th Armored Brigade	1-29-1968	1-13-1974
	40th Infantry Division	1-13-1974	
3-185	40th Armored Division	7-1-1959	1-29-1968
	185th Armor Group	1-29-1968	10-1-1971
	California	10-1-1971	1-13-1974
	40th Infantry Division	1-13-1974	8-1-1997
4-185	40th Armored Division	7-1-1959	1-29-1968
5-185	40th Armored Division	7-1-1959	1-29-1968
6-185	California	5-1-1962	3-1-1963
	Attached-40th Armored Division	3-1-1963	1-29-1968
7-185	California	5-1-1962	3-1-1963

186th Armored Regiment-National Guard

| 3-186 | 34th Infantry Division | | |

187th Armored Regiment-National Guard

1-187	48th Armored Division		7-1-1959	4-16-1963
	53rd Infantry Brigade		4-16-1963	3-1-1964
	53rd Armored Brigade		3-1-1964	1-20-1968

192nd Cavalry Regiment-National Guard

1-192	29th Infantry Division	RSTA		
E-192	92nd Infantry Brigade		5-1-1964	

194th Armored Regiment-National Guard

1-194	47th Infantry Division	ARM	2-22-1959	2-10-1991
	34th Infantry Division	CAV	2-10-1991	9-1-1992
	34th Infantry Division	ARM	10-1-2000	
2-194	47th Infantry Division	ARM	2-22-1959	1-1-1972
	34th Infantry Division	ARM	9-1-2002	
3-194	34th Infantry Division	ARM		

195th Armored Regiment-National Guard

1-195	67th Infantry Brigade		5-1-1968	10-1-1985
	35th Infantry Division		10-1-1985	10-1-2000

196th Cavalry Regiment-National Guard

1-196	30th Infantry Division		4-1-1959	12-1-1973
2-196	30th Infantry Division		4-1-1959	3-10-1963
E-196	30th Infantry Brigade		12-1-1973	9-1-2002
	30th Armored Brigade		9-1-2002	

198th Armored Regiment-National Guard

1-198	31st Infantry Division		5-2-1959	2-15-1968
	30th Armored Division		2-15-1968	11-1-1973
	155th Armored Brigade		11-1-1973	
	36th Infantry Division			
2-198	31st Infantry Division		5-2-1959	2-15-1968
	30th Armored Division		2-15-1968	11-1-1973
	155th Armored Brigade		11-1-1973	

202nd Cavalry Regiment-National Guard

| B-202 | 218th Infantry Brigade | 10-1-1991 | |

203rd Armored Regiment-National Guard

1-203	35th Infantry Division	4-15-1959	4-1-1963
	Missouri	4-1-1963	2-1-1968
2-203	35th Infantry Division	4-15-1959	4-1-1963
	Missouri	4-1-1963	2-1-1968

205th Armored Regiment-National Guard

| 1-205 | 27th Armored Division | 3-16-1959 | 2-1-1968 |

206th Armored Regiment-National Guard

| 1-206 | 39th Infantry Division | 7-1-1959 | 12-1-1967 |
| 2-206 | 39th Infantry Division | 5-1-1963 | 12-1-1967 |

208th Armored Regiment-National Guard

| 1-208 | 27th Armored Division | 3-16-1959 | 2-1-1968 |

210th Armored Regiment-National Guard

1-210	27th Armored Division	10-1-1960	2-1-1968
	New York	2-1-1968	4-1-1986
	42nd Infantry Division	4-1-1986	9-1-1993
2-210	Middletown New York	- -1989	- -1989

221st Cavalry Regiment-National Guard

1-221	40th Infantry Division	4-1-1980	9-1-1995
	Las Vegas Nevada	9-1-1995	9-1-1997
	11th Armored Cavalry	9-1-1997	Present

223rd Cavalry Regiment-National Guard

1-223	28th Infantry Division		4-1-1963	4-1-1975

230th Cavalry Regiment-National Guard

1-230	30th Armored Division		4-1-1963	11-1-1973
A-230	30th Armored Brigade		11-1-1973	1-1-1980
B-230	30th Armored Brigade		1-1-1980	9-1-1996

237th Cavalry Regiment-National Guard

1-237	37th Infantry Division		4-1-1963	2-1-1968
A-237	73rd Infantry Brigade		3-1-1977	9-1-1992
	37th Infantry Brigade		9-1-1992	9-1-1993

238th Cavalry Regiment-National Guard

1-238	38th Infantry Division		3-1-1963	9-1-1994
	38th Infantry Division	RSTA		
E-238	76th Infantry Brigade		9-1-1994	

240th Cavalry Regiment-National Guard

A-240	149th Armored Brigade		11-01-1980	11-1-1985

245th Armored Regiment-National Guard

1-245	45th Infantry Division		5-1-1959	1-2-1968
2-245	45th Infantry Division		5-1-1959	1-2-1968

246th Armored Regiment-National Guard

1-246	46th Infantry Division		3-15-1959	3-15-1963
	38th Infantry Division		2-1-1968	10-1-1999
2-246	46th Infantry Division		3-15-1959	2-1-1968
3-246	46th Infantry Division		3-15-1963	2-1-1968

252nd Armored Regiment-National Guard

1-252	30th Infantry Division		3-10-1963	11-30-1973
	30th Infantry Brigade		11-30-1973	9-1-2002
	30th Armored Brigade		9-1-2002	
	29th Infantry Division			
2-252	30th Infantry Division		3-10-1963	11-30-1973
	North Carolina		11-30-1973	9-1-1996

256th Cavalry Regiment-National Guard

| E-256 | 256th Infantry Brigade | | 12-16-1967 | 9-2-1995 |

263rd Cavalry Regiment-National Guard

1-263	51st Infantry Division		4-1-1959	4-1-1963
	Mullins South Carolina		4-1-1963	10-1-1995
	218th Infantry Brigade		10-1-1995	
	35th Infantry Division	RSTA		
2-263	51st Infantry Division		4-1-1959	4-1-1963
	53rd Infantry Brigade		4-1-1963	2-1-1964
	53rd Armored Brigade		2-1-1964	1-1-1968
	30th Infantry Division		1-1-1968	11-30-1973
	218th Infantry Brigade		11-30-1973	10-1-1995
3-263	South Carolina		4-30-1964	1-1-1968

278th Cavalry Regiment-National Guard

1-278	Athens Tennessee	ACR	5-1-1977	
	38th Infantry Division	RSTA		
2-278	Kingsport Tennessee	ACR	5-1-1977	
3-278	Cookeville Tennessee	ACR	2-1-1980	
4-278	Smyrna Tennessee	Sup		

279th Cavalry Regiment-National Guard

| 1-279 | 35th Infantry Division | RSTA | | |

303rd Armored Regiment-National Guard

1-303	41st Infantry Division		4-1-1959	3-1-1968
	Washington		3-1-1968	4-1-1971
	81st Infantry Brigade		4-1-1971	8-1-2000

148

Unit	Assignment		From	To
	81st Armored Brigade		8-1-2000	
2-303	41st Infantry Division		3-1-1963	3-1-1968

303rd Cavalry Regiment-National Guard

Unit	Assignment		From	To
1-303	40th Infantry Division	RSTA		
E-303	81st Infantry Brigade		3-1-1968	8-1-2000
	81st Armored Brigade		8-1-2000	

348th Cavalry Regiment-National Guard

Unit	Assignment	From	To
1-348	38th Infantry Brigade	11-30-1973	9-2-1995

632nd Armored Regiment-National Guard

Unit	Assignment	From	To
1-632	32nd Infantry Division	4-1-1963	12-30-1967
	264th Armor Group	12-30-1967	1-1-1972
	32nd Infantry Brigade	1-1-1972	9-1-1997
	34th Infantry Division	9-1-1997	9-1-2001
2-632	32nd Infantry Division	4-1-1963	12-30-1967

635th Armored Regiment-National Guard

Unit	Assignment	From	To
1-635	69th Infantry Brigade	2-1-1976	3-1-1990
	35th Infantry Division	3-1-1990	10-1-1999
	40th Infantry Division	10-1-1999	
2-635	35th Infantry Division	3-1-1990	9-1-1997

713th Cavalry Regiment-National Guard

Unit	Assignment	From	To
B-713	218th Infantry Brigade	1-1-1974	10-1-1991
E-713	218th Infantry Brigade	1-1-1974	

748th Cavalry Regiment-National Guard

Unit	Assignment	From	To
1-748	48th Armored Division	4-16-1963	1-1-1968

803rd Armored Regiment-National Guard

Unit	Assignment	From	To
1-803	Everett Washington	1-1-1974	9-1-1993